NOTE

1. All recipes serve four unless otherwise stated.

2. All spoon measurements are level.

3. All eggs are sizes 3 or 4 unless otherwise stated.

4. Preparation times given are an average calculated during recipe testing.

5. Metric and imperial measurements have been calculated separately. Use one set of measurements only as they are not exact equivalents.

6. Cooking times may vary slightly depending on the individual oven. Dishes should be placed in the centre of the oven unless otherwise specified.

7. Always preheat the oven or grill to the specified temperature.

8. Spoon measures can be bought in both imperial and metric sizes to give accurate measurement of small quantities.

Just Desserts

Just Desserts

Jeni Wright

TREASURE PRESS

Contents

First published in Great Britain in 1980 by
Hennerwood Publications Ltd

This edition published in 1985 by
Treasure Press
59 Grosvenor Street
London W1

Reprinted 1985

ISBN 1 85051 069 5

Printed in Hong Kong

WINTER PUDDINGS

Winter is the time of year to indulge in satisfying, substantial puddings. When it's cold outside, there's nothing more warming than a piping hot steamed pudding, or a crisply baked double crust fruit pie. It's the time of year when most people, even confirmed non-pudding eaters, usually feel the need for that something extra at the end of a meal, and so a pudding in wintertime is considered a real treat. Use this chapter as a store of ideas to inspire you through the long winter months, to cheer up family and friends in even the gloomiest of weather.

Orange marmalade sponge pudding

Metric	Imperial
2×15 ml spoons marmalade	2 tablespoons marmalade
175 g self-raising flour	6 oz self-raising flour
100 g caster sugar	4 oz caster sugar
100 g soft (tub) margarine	4 oz soft (tub) margarine
2 eggs, lightly beaten	2 eggs, lightly beaten
finely grated rind and juice of 1 large orange	finely grated rind and juice of 1 large orange

Sauce:	Sauce:
1×15 ml spoon cornflour	1 tablespoon cornflour
300 ml water	½ pint water
2×15 ml spoons marmalade	2 tablespoons marmalade
2×15 ml spoons dark soft brown sugar	2 tablespoons dark soft brown sugar

Spread the marmalade in the bottom of a buttered 1.2 litre/2 pint pudding basin. Sift the flour into a bowl. Add the sugar, margarine and eggs, then beat for 2 to 3 minutes until the mixture is soft and light. Add the orange rind and juice and beat again until thoroughly mixed together.

Spoon the mixture into the basin, then cover the top of the basin with greased foil. Make a pleat in the centre to allow the pudding to rise during steaming. Tie securely with string.

Place the basin in the top of a steamer or double boiler, or in a pan half-filled with gently bubbling water. Cover with a lid, then steam for 2 hours, topping up the water level in the pan as necessary.

Meanwhile, make the sauce: mix the cornflour to a paste in a pan with a little of the water, then stir in the remaining water, the marmalade and sugar. Bring slowly to the boil, stirring constantly, then lower the heat and simmer until thick and glossy.

Remove the foil from the basin, then turn the pudding out carefully on to a warmed serving dish. Pour a little sauce over the pudding, then hand the rest separately. Serve hot.
Serves 4 to 6

Individual cherry puddings

Metric	Imperial
6×15 ml spoons golden syrup	6 tablespoons golden syrup
100 g glacé cherries	4 oz glacé cherries
75 g plain flour	3 oz plain flour
1×5 ml spoon baking powder	1 teaspoon baking powder
pinch of salt	pinch of salt
75 g fresh white breadcrumbs	3 oz fresh white breadcrumbs
75 g shredded suet	3 oz shredded suet
40 g caster sugar	1½ oz caster sugar
1 small egg, beaten	1 small egg, beaten
6-8×15 ml spoons milk	6-8 tablespoons milk

These attractive little puddings will be much appreciated by children, and the steaming time is almost halved by using individual moulds rather than a large pudding basin.

Put 1×15 ml spoon/1 tablespoon golden syrup in the bottom of each of 6 buttered individual dariole moulds. Cut about 18 cherries in half, then place them cut sides uppermost in the bottom of the moulds. Chop the remaining cherries roughly and set aside.

Sift the flour, baking powder and salt into a bowl. Add the breadcrumbs, suet and sugar and stir until evenly mixed, then stir in the reserved chopped cherries and the egg. Beat well to mix, adding enough milk to give a soft dropping consistency. Divide the mixture equally between the dariole moulds.

Cover the tops of the puddings with circles of buttered greaseproof paper, then cover the tops of the moulds with foil, making pleats in the centre to allow for the puddings to rise during steaming. Tie securely with string.

Place the moulds in the top of a steamer or double boiler, or in a pan half-filled with gently bubbling water. Cover with a lid, then steam for 1 hour, topping up the water level in the pan as necessary.

Remove the foil and greaseproof paper, then turn the puddings out carefully on to a warmed serving dish. Serve hot, with thin pouring custard or cream.
Makes 6

Orange marmalade sponge pudding;
Individual cherry puddings

Original frangipane flan

Cooking time: 50 minutes to an hour
Oven: 190°C, 375°F, Gas Mark 5

Metric
1 ×225 g packet frozen puff
 pastry, thawed
3 ×15 ml spoons apricot jam
100 g butter, softened
100 g caster sugar
2 eggs, lightly beaten
100 g ground almonds

Imperial
1 ×8 oz packet frozen puff
 pastry, thawed
3 tablespoons apricot jam
4 oz butter, softened
4 oz caster sugar
2 eggs, lightly beaten
4 oz ground almonds

To finish:
50 g icing sugar, sifted
1-2 ×5 ml spoons hot water

To finish:
2 oz icing sugar, sifted
1-2 teaspoons hot water

This flan is also excellent served cold at teatime.

Roll out the pastry on a lightly floured surface and use it to line a lightly buttered 20 cm/8 inch flan dish or sandwich tin. Reserve the pastry trimmings. Spread the jam over the pastry.

Put the butter and sugar in a bowl and beat together until light and fluffy. Add the eggs a little at a time, beating well, then beat in the almonds.

Spread the mixture over the jam in the dish or tin. Roll out the reserved pastry trimmings into strips long enough to go across the flan, then arrange them over the top and seal the ends with water. Bake in a preheated oven for 40 to 45 minutes or until the filling is set.

Meanwhile, beat the icing sugar and water together to make a smooth glacé icing. Remove the flan from the oven, brush with the icing, then return to the oven. Bake for a further 5 minutes, then leave to cool for 10 minutes before serving. Serve warm or cold.
Serves 6 to 8

Original frangipane flan

Apple oat Betty; Indian sweet rice

Apple oat Betty

Metric
75 g plain flour
pinch of salt
2×5 ml spoons ground
   cinnamon
75 g rolled oats
100 g demerara sugar
100 g butter or margarine
450 g cooking apples
2×15 ml spoons apricot jam
finely grated rind and juice
   of 1 lemon

Imperial
3 oz plain flour
pinch of salt
2 teaspoons ground
   cinnamon
3 oz rolled oats
4 oz demerara sugar
4 oz butter or margarine
1 lb cooking apples
2 tablespoons apricot jam
finely grated rind and juice
   of 1 lemon

Cooking time: 50 minutes to 1 hour
Oven: 190°C, 375°F, Gas Mark 5

Sift the flour, salt and half the cinnamon into a bowl. Stir in the oats and sugar. Add 75 g/3 oz of the butter or margarine in pieces, then rub into the dry ingredients until evenly mixed.
Peel, core and slice the apples thinly, then mix with the jam and the remaining cinnamon. Put half the apples in the bottom of a buttered baking dish. Sprinkle with half the lemon rind and juice, then half the oat mixture. Repeat these layers once more, finishing with a layer of oat mixture, then dot with the remaining butter.
Bake in a preheated oven for 50 minutes to 1 hour until the topping is crisp and the apples feel tender when pierced with a skewer. Serve hot, with custard.

Indian sweet rice

Metric
100 g short-grain rice
50 g desiccated coconut
50 g slivered or flaked
   almonds
50 g sultanas or seedless
   raisins
50 g granulated sugar
900 ml milk
1×15 ml spoon rosewater
   (optional)

Imperial
4 oz short-grain rice
2 oz desiccated coconut
2 oz slivered or flaked
   almonds
2 oz sultanas or seedless
   raisins
2 oz granulated sugar
1½ pints milk
1 tablespoon rosewater
   (optional)

Cooking time: 1 to 1¼ hours
Oven: 220°C, 425°F, Gas Mark 7; reduced to
      140°C, 275°F, Gas Mark 1

Spread the rice evenly in the bottom of a large baking dish. Cover with the coconut, then the almonds, sultanas or raisins and sugar. Pour in 600 ml/1 pint milk, then bake in a preheated oven for 30 minutes. Lower the heat to cool, then add the remaining milk. Bake for a further 30 to 45 minutes or until the rice is tender. Sprinkle over the rosewater (if using). Serve immediately.
Serves 6

Christmas pudding

Metric
450 g fresh white
    breadcrumbs
225 g shredded suet
225 g dark molasses sugar
1×5 ml spoon ground ginger
1×5 ml spoon ground
    cinnamon
1×2.5 ml spoon salt
225 g seedless raisins
225 g sultanas
225 g currants
50 g mixed candied peel,
    chopped
50 g glacé cherries,
    chopped
50 g blanched almonds,
    chopped
1 cooking apple, peeled,
    cored and grated
2×15 ml spoons golden
    syrup
2×15 ml spoons brandy
3 eggs, lightly beaten
150 ml milk, to mix

Imperial
1 lb fresh white
    breadcrumbs
8 oz shredded suet
8 oz dark molasses sugar
1 teaspoon ground ginger
1 teaspoon ground
    cinnamon
½ teaspoon salt
8 oz seedless raisins
8 oz sultanas
8 oz currants
2 oz mixed candied peel,
    chopped
2 oz glacé cherries,
    chopped
2 oz blanched almonds,
    chopped
1 cooking apple, peeled,
    cored and grated
2 tablespoons golden
    syrup
2 tablespoons brandy
3 eggs, lightly beaten
¼ pint milk, to mix

This is a light-textured pudding which is usually more popular with children than the heavier, traditional kind of Christmas pudding. It is also a useful recipe because it should be made only a few days before required – it does not need a long maturing time. Remember, however, to start preparing the ingredients the day before steaming, as the mixture improves if left to stand overnight.

Put all the dry ingredients in a bowl and stir well to mix. Add the apple, golden syrup, brandy and eggs, then enough milk to give a soft dropping consistency. Cover and leave to stand overnight.
The next day, spoon the mixture into buttered pudding basins, pressing it down well. Leave room for the puddings to rise during steaming. Cover with circles of buttered greaseproof paper, then cover with pudding cloth or foil and tie securely with string.
Place the puddings in the top of a steamer or double boiler, or in a pan half-filled with gently bubbling water. Cover with a lid, then steam for 8 hours, topping up the water level in the pan as necessary.
Remove the puddings from the pan and discard the cloth or foil and the greaseproof paper. Leave until cold, then cover with fresh greaseproof and cloth or foil. Store in a cool dry place for up to 1 week, then steam again for 2 to 3 hours before serving.
Makes 2×1 kg/2 lb puddings

Christmas pudding; Old-fashioned plum pudding

Old-fashioned plum pudding

Metric	Imperial
225 g self-raising flour	*8 oz self-raising flour*
2 × 5 ml spoons ground mixed spice	*2 teaspoons ground mixed spice*
1 × 5 ml spoon salt	*1 teaspoon salt*
450 g shredded suet	*1 lb shredded suet*
225 g fresh white breadcrumbs	*8 oz fresh white breadcrumbs*
450 g dark soft brown sugar	*1 lb dark soft brown sugar*
450 g seedless raisins	*1 lb seedless raisins*
450 g sultanas	*1 lb sultanas*
450 g currants	*1 lb currants*
100 g mixed candied peel, chopped	*4 oz mixed candied peel, chopped*
100 g glacé cherries, chopped (optional)	*4 oz glacé cherries chopped (optional)*
2 medium carrots, peeled and grated	*2 medium carrots, peeled and grated*
6 eggs, beaten	*6 eggs, beaten*
150 ml sweet stout or brandy	*¼ pint sweet stout or brandy*
2 × 15 ml spoons black treacle	*2 tablespoons black treacle*
finely grated rind and juice of 1 orange	*finely grated rind and juice of 1 orange*
finely grated rind and juice of 1 lemon	*finely grated rind and juice of 1 lemon*

This is a traditional recipe for Christmas pudding, which is both dark and heavy and will benefit from long keeping. For best results at Christmas time, make the puddings about eight weeks in advance. After steaming, remove the greaseproof paper and the cloth or foil, then replace with fresh greaseproof paper and clean pudding cloth. Tie securely with string and store in a cool, dry place.

While it is perfectly safe to steam the puddings covered with foil, it is advisable *not* to store them covered with foil. Sometimes there is a tendency for the fruit in the puddings to react with the foil and this can result in the puddings becoming mouldy, particularly if they are not stored in ideal conditions.

Sift the flour into a bowl with the mixed spice and salt. Stir in the suet, breadcrumbs and sugar, then add the dried fruit, candied peel, cherries (if using) and the carrots. Stir well to mix, then add the eggs, stout or brandy, black treacle and the orange and lemon rinds and juice. Beat until thoroughly combined.

Spoon the mixture into buttered pudding basins, pressing it down well. Leave room for the puddings to rise during steaming. Cover with circles of buttered greaseproof paper, then cover with pudding cloth or foil and tie securely with string.

Place the puddings in the top of a steamer or double boiler, or in a pan half-filled with gently bubbling water. Cover with a lid, then steam for 8 hours, topping up the water level in the pan as necessary.

Remove the puddings from the pan and discard the cloth or foil and the greaseproof paper. Leave until cold, then cover with fresh greaseproof and cloth (see introduction). Store in a cool, dry place until required; then steam again for 2 to 3 hours before serving.

Makes 5 × 450 g/1 lb puddings

Orange and date fruit salad; Winter prune fool

Orange and date fruit salad

Metric	Imperial
100 g granulated sugar	4 oz granulated sugar
150 ml water	¼ pint water
1 × 1.25 ml spoon vanilla essence	¼ teaspoon vanilla essence
2 oranges, peeled, pipped and sliced into rings	2 oranges, peeled, pipped and sliced into rings
75 g whole dates, stoned and chopped	3 oz whole dates, stoned and chopped
100 g green grapes, halved and seeded	4 oz green grapes, halved and seeded
2 dessert apples	2 dessert apples
juice of ½ lemon	juice of ½ lemon
50 g slivered or flaked almonds	2 oz slivered or flaked almonds

Put the sugar, water and vanilla essence in a heavy pan and heat gently until the sugar has dissolved. Bring to the boil and boil rapidly for 2 minutes or until syrupy, then remove from the heat and leave to cool.

Put the orange rings in a serving bowl with the dates and grapes. Peel and core the apples, then cut into thin slices. Add to the fruit in the bowl and sprinkle with the lemon juice to prevent discolouration. Pour over the cooled sugar syrup, then stir gently to mix. Sprinkle with the nuts. Serve cold, with cream if liked.

Winter prune fool

Metric	Imperial
100 g pitted prunes, soaked overnight in cold water	4 oz pitted prunes, soaked overnight in cold water
50 g caster sugar	2 oz caster sugar
juice of 1 orange	juice of 1 orange
2 × 15 ml spoons redcurrant jelly	2 tablespoons redcurrant jelly
1 × 15 ml spoon custard powder	1 tablespoon custard powder
150 ml milk	¼ pint milk
150 ml whipping or double cream	¼ pint whipping or double cream
25-50 g chopped nuts (walnuts, almonds, etc), to finish	1-2 oz chopped nuts (walnuts, almonds, etc), to finish

Fruit fools are usually associated with soft summer fruits, but there is no reason why they cannot be made in the winter with dried fruit. Dried apricots or figs could be substituted for the prunes used here.

Drain the prunes, then chop the flesh roughly. Put in a pan with the sugar, orange juice and redcurrant jelly, then heat gently for 10 minutes until soft, stirring occasionally.

Meanwhile, mix the custard powder to a paste with a little of the milk. Heat the remaining milk to just below boiling point, then stir slowly into the custard paste. Return to the pan and cook until the custard is very thick, stirring constantly. Leave to cool.

Reduce the prune mixture to a smooth purée in a liquidizer, then fold into the cooled custard. Whip the cream until thick, then fold into the prune custard until evenly blended. Spoon into individual glasses or bowls, then chill in the refrigerator until firm. Sprinkle with the chopped nuts. Serve chilled.

Steamed apricot and apple mould

Metric
175 g self-raising flour
pinch of salt
50 g caster sugar
75 g shredded suet
about 5×15 ml spoons milk

Imperial
6 oz self-raising flour
pinch of salt
2 oz caster sugar
3 oz shredded suet
about 5 tablespoons milk

Filling:
1 cooking apple
175 g dried apricots, soaked
    overnight in cold water
50 g seedless raisins
1×2.5 ml spoon ground
    mixed spice
3×15 ml spoons golden
    syrup
2-3×15 ml spoons demerara
    sugar, to finish

Filling:
1 cooking apple
6 oz dried apricots, soaked
    overnight in cold water
2 oz seedless raisins
½ teaspoon ground
    mixed spice
3 tablespoons golden
    syrup
2-3 tablespoons demerara
    sugar, to finish

To make the pastry: sift the flour and salt into a bowl. Stir in the sugar and suet, then add the milk gradually and knead lightly to form a firm dough. Wrap in foil, then chill in the refrigerator while making the filling.
To make the filling: peel and core the apple, then grate it into a bowl. Drain the apricots and chop them finely, then stir in with the remaining filling ingredients using 3×15 ml spoons/3 tablespoons of the syrup.
Roll out the dough on a lightly floured surface, then cut out a small circle large enough to fit the base of a well-buttered 900 ml/1½ pint pudding basin. Place the dough in the basin, then cover with a layer of filling. Continue cutting out circles of dough and layering them with the filling until all the ingredients are used up, making 4 layers of dough and 3 of filling.
Cover the top of the pudding with a circle of buttered greaseproof paper, then cover the top of the basin with foil, making a pleat in the centre to allow for the pastry to rise during steaming. Tie securely with string.
Place the basin in the top of a steamer or double boiler, or in a pan half-filled with gently bubbling water. Cover with a lid, then steam for 2 hours.
Remove the foil and greaseproof paper, then leave the pudding to stand in the basin for 5 minutes. Turn out carefully on to a warmed serving dish and sprinkle liberally with demerara sugar. Serve hot, with thin pouring custard or cream.
Serves 4 to 6

Steamed apricot and apple mould

Rich chocolate meringue pie

Metric
175 g plain flour
pinch of salt
75 g butter or margarine
about 2×15 ml spoons
 water

Filling:
300 ml milk
100 g plain chocolate,
 broken into pieces
100 g soft brown sugar
3×15 ml spoons plain flour
50 g butter or margarine
2 egg yolks, lightly beaten

Topping:
2 egg whites
3×15 ml spoons icing sugar,
 sifted

Imperial
6 oz plain flour
pinch of salt
3 oz butter or margarine
about 2 tablespoons
 water

Filling:
½ pint milk
4 oz plain chocolate, broken
 into pieces
4 oz soft brown sugar
3 tablespoons plain flour
2 oz butter or margarine
2 egg yolks, lightly beaten

Topping:
2 egg whites
3 tablespoons icing sugar,
 sifted

Rich chocolate meringue pie;
Rich chocolate pudding with hot fudge sauce

Cooking time: 40 minutes
Oven: 200°C, 400°F, Gas Mark 6; reduced to
 140°C, 275°F, Gas Mark 1

It is important to use plain flour when making the chocolate filling for this pie.

To make the pastry: sift the flour and salt into a bowl. Add the butter or margarine in pieces, then rub into the flour with the fingertips until the mixture resembles fine breadcrumbs. Stir in the water gradually and mix to a firm dough. Chill for 30 minutes.
Roll out the dough on a lightly floured surface and use it to line a 20 cm/8 inch flan dish or flan ring placed on a baking sheet. Fill with foil and baking beans, then bake 'blind' in a preheated moderately hot oven for 15 minutes. Remove the foil and beans, then bake for a further 10 minutes.
Meanwhile, make the filling: put the milk and chocolate in a heavy pan and heat gently until the chocolate has melted, stirring frequently. Put the remaining filling ingredients in a bowl and mix well together. Pour on the hot milk and chocolate mixture, stir well to mix, then return the mixture to the pan. Bring slowly to the boil, stirring with a wooden spoon.
Lower the heat and continue cooking until the mixture is thick and dark, stirring constantly. Remove the pan from the heat and leave the mixture to cool for 5 minutes, then pour into the baked flan case.
Beat the egg whites until stiff, then add the icing sugar and beat again until glossy. Spoon or pipe the meringue over the chocolate filling to cover it completely, then bake in the cool oven for 15 minutes or until the meringue is golden. Leave until completely cold.
Serves 6

Rich chocolate pudding with hot fudge sauce

Metric
100 g plain chocolate
4×15 ml spoons milk
100 g butter or margarine
100 g soft brown sugar
1 egg, separated
75 g fresh white
   breadcrumbs
75 g self-raising flour

Hot fudge sauce:
25 g plain chocolate, broken
   into pieces
15 g butter or margarine
1×175 g can evaporated
   milk
50 g soft brown sugar
2×15 ml spoons golden
   syrup

Imperial
4 oz plain chocolate
4 tablespoons milk
4 oz butter or margarine
4 oz soft brown sugar
1 egg, separated
3 oz fresh white
   breadcrumbs
3 oz self-raising flour

Hot fudge sauce:
1 oz plain chocolate, broken
   into pieces
½ oz butter or margarine
1×6 oz can evaporated
   milk
2 oz soft brown sugar
2 tablespoons golden
   syrup

Cooking time: 2 to 2½ hours

To make the pudding: put half the chocolate in a heatproof bowl with the milk. Stand the bowl in a pan of gently simmering water and heat until the chocolate has melted, stirring occasionally. Grate the remaining chocolate and set aside.

Put the butter or margarine and sugar in a separate bowl and beat until soft. Beat in the melted chocolate, then the egg yolk. Add the breadcrumbs and flour and beat again until well mixed.

Beat the egg white until stiff, then fold into the pudding mixture with the reserved grated chocolate. Spoon the mixture into a buttered 1.2 litre/2 pint pudding basin. Cover the top of the pudding with a circle of buttered greaseproof paper, then cover the top of the basin with foil, making a pleat in the centre to allow the pudding to rise during steaming. Tie securely with string.

Place the basin in the top of a steamer or double boiler, or in a pan half-filled with gently bubbling water. Cover with a lid, then steam for 2 to 2½ hours, topping up the water level in the pan as necessary.

Meanwhile, make the fudge sauce: put all the ingredients in a heavy pan and heat gently until melted. Bring to the boil, then lower the heat and simmer for about 5 minutes or until thick and glossy.

Remove the foil and greaseproof paper from the pudding, then turn it out carefully on to a warmed serving dish. Pour a little hot fudge sauce over the pudding, then pour the remaining sauce into a jug and hand separately. Serve immediately.
Serves 6

Mincemeat and apple roll

Metric	Imperial
1×225 g packet frozen puff pastry, thawed	1×8 oz packet frozen puff pastry, thawed
15 g butter, melted	½ oz butter, melted
1 large cooking apple	1 large cooking apple
juice of ½ lemon	juice of ½ lemon
3×15 ml spoons mincemeat	3 tablespoons mincemeat
50 g caster sugar	2 oz caster sugar
1×1.25 ml spoon ground cinnamon	¼ teaspoon ground cinnamon

To finish:	To finish:
1 small egg, beaten	1 small egg, beaten
1×15 ml spoon caster sugar	1 tablespoon caster sugar
1×1.25 ml spoon ground cinnamon	¼ teaspoon ground cinnamon

Cooking time: 30 minutes
Oven: 200°C, 400°F, Gas Mark 6

This is an economical pudding because the puff pastry makes a small amount of filling go a long way.

Roll out the pastry on a lightly floured surface to a rectangle about 30×20 cm/12×8 inches. Brush with the melted butter.
Peel, core and grate the apple, then mix with the lemon juice, mincemeat, sugar and cinnamon. Spread this mixture over the pastry, leaving a 1 cm/½ inch margin around the edges.
Roll up the pastry from the long end to form a Swiss roll shape, sealing the join with a little water. Stand the roll on a damp baking sheet with the join underneath, then brush all over with the beaten egg. Sprinkle with the sugar and cinnamon.
Bake in a preheated oven for about 30 minutes or until golden. Leave to stand for 5 minutes, then cut into slices. Serve warm with cream or custard.

Variation:
Omit the mincemeat and add 50 g/2 oz dried, stoned apricots, soaked overnight, drained and chopped and added with the apple.

Omit the mincemeat and add 50 g/2 oz chopped stoned dates with the apple.

Apricot and almond bake

Metric	Imperial
15 g butter or margarine, softened	½ oz butter or margarine, softened
1×750 g can apricot halves, drained	1×1¾ lb can apricot halves, drained
50 g ground almonds	2 oz ground almonds
100 g fresh white breadcrumbs	4 oz fresh white breadcrumbs
300 ml milk	½ pint milk
1 egg	1 egg
1 egg yolk	1 egg yolk
1×2.5 ml spoon grated nutmeg	½ teaspoon grated nutmeg
50 g demerara sugar	2 oz demerara sugar

Cooking time: 1 hour
Oven: 190°C, 375°F, Gas Mark 5

When fresh apricots are in season these may be used instead of the canned ones suggested here. Use about 750 g/1½ lb apricots, halve them and remove the stones before cooking.

Brush the inside of a 1.2 litre/2 pint ovenproof dish with the butter or margarine. Arrange a layer of apricot halves in the bottom of the dish, cut side down. Sprinkle with a layer of almonds, then with a layer of breadcrumbs. Continue with these layers until all the ingredients are used up, reserving the last layer of breadcrumbs.
Beat together the milk, egg, egg yolk and half the nutmeg, then pour into the dish. Mix together the reserved breadcrumbs, the sugar and remaining nutmeg and sprinkle over the top of the pudding.
Bake in a preheated oven for 1 hour until the topping is crisp and golden brown. Serve hot, with cream or thin pouring custard.
Serves 4 to 6

Apricot and almond bake; Mincemeat and apple roll

16

Canadian raisin pie

Metric	Imperial
175 g soft brown sugar	6 oz soft brown sugar
2×15 ml spoons plain flour	2 tablespoons plain flour
pinch of salt	pinch of salt
350 g seedless raisins	12 oz seedless raisins
450 ml water	¾ pint water
2×15 ml spoons maple or golden syrup	2 tablespoons maple or golden syrup
finely grated rind and juice of 1 lemon	finely grated rind and juice of 1 lemon

Pastry:	Pastry:
275 g plain flour	10 oz plain flour
pinch of salt	pinch of salt
2×5 ml spoons baking powder	2 teaspoons baking powder
75 g caster sugar	3 oz caster sugar
1×1.25 ml spoon vanilla essence	¼ teaspoon vanilla essence
1 egg, separated	1 egg, separated
1×15 ml spoon milk	1 tablespoon milk
150 g butter or margarine	5 oz butter or margarine

Cooking time: 30 minutes
Oven: 200°C, 400°F, Gas Mark 6

It is well worth making Raisin Pie in such a large quantity as this, as it is just as good served cold as hot, and it makes an unusual alternative to mince pie at Christmas time. The rich sweet pastry case is crisp and light when hot, yet slightly soft when cold. If preferred, individual pies can be made in the usual way. This will make about 30 pies.

To make the filling: put all the ingredients in a pan. Bring to the boil, then lower the heat and simmer for about 10 minutes until the raisins are plump and the mixture is thick, stirring frequently. Remove from the heat and leave to cool.
Meanwhile, make the pastry: sift the flour, salt and baking powder into a bowl. Make a well in the centre, put in the sugar, vanilla essence, half the egg yolk, and all the egg white and milk. Stir the ingredients together until evenly mixed, then add the butter or margarine in pieces and beat quickly into the flour mixture. Knead lightly to form a smooth dough, wrap in foil and chill in the refrigerator for 30 minutes.
Roll out the dough on a lightly floured surface, and use half to line a 23 cm/9 inch flan dish. Spoon the filling into the dish, then cover with the remaining dough. Prick the top dough with a fork, then brush with the remaining egg yolk mixed with a little milk. Bake in a preheated oven for 30 minutes or until the pastry is golden brown. Remove from the oven and leave to cool for 15 minutes. Serve warm or cold.
Serves 8

Three fruit charlotte

Metric	Imperial
3 large oranges, peel and pith removed	3 large oranges, peel and pith removed
1 lemon, peel and pith removed	1 lemon, peel and pith removed
100 g granulated sugar	4 oz granulated sugar
2×15 ml spoons marmalade	2 tablespoons marmalade
2 medium cooking apples	2 medium cooking apples
about 12 slices of white bread, crusts removed	about 12 slices of white bread, crusts removed
100-175 g butter or margarine, softened	4-6 oz butter or margarine, softened

Cooking time: 1 hour
Oven: 190°C, 375°F, Gas Mark 5

If you don't have a charlotte mould use a 1.2 litre/2 pint pudding basin.

Chop the flesh of the oranges and lemon and put in a pan with their juice; then add the sugar and marmalade. Heat gently until the sugar has dissolved, then bring to the boil and boil rapidly until the fruit is soft and the juice is thick and syrupy. Peel, core and slice the apples, then add to the pan and cook for a few minutes until just tender but still whole.
Spread the bread generously with some of the butter or margarine, then arrange about 5 slices around the inside of a buttered 1.2 litre/2 pint charlotte mould, overlapping the slices slightly. Put 1 to 2 slices of bread in the bottom of the mould to cover it completely.
Spread half the fruit mixture over the bread in the bottom of the mould, then cover with 1 to 2 more slices of bread. Repeat these 2 layers once more, ending with a layer of bread, then press down firmly and spread the top of the charlotte with some more of the butter or margarine.
Bake in a preheated oven for 50 minutes, then turn out on to a baking sheet and spread the remaining butter or margarine all over the charlotte. Return the charlotte to the oven and bake for a further 10 minutes until crisp. Serve hot, with fresh pouring cream.

Canadian raisin pie; Three fruit charlotte; Toast and butter pudding

Toast and butter pudding

Cooking time: 40 minutes
Oven: 190°C, 375°F, Gas Mark 5

This is a good way to use leftover toast from breakfast, or stale bread. Any proportion of dried fruit can be used instead of those suggested here, and for convenience, you can also use the mixed dried fruit sold in packages for cake making.

Mix together the dried fruit, peel, orange rind and juice. Put half this mixture in the bottom of a buttered baking dish. Spread the toast with the butter or margarine, then cut into small pieces. Cover the fruit with half the toast and sprinkle with half the sugar. Repeat these layers once more.

Mix together the milk, eggs and cinnamon and pour into the dish. Leave to soak for 1 to 2 hours. Bake in a preheated oven for about 40 minutes until crisp on top. Serve hot, with thin pouring custard.

Metric	*Imperial*
50 g seedless raisins	*2 oz seedless raisins*
50 g currants	*2 oz currants*
50 g sultanas	*2 oz sultanas*
50 g chopped mixed peel	*2 oz chopped mixed peel*
finely grated rind and juice of 1 orange	*finely grated rind and juice of 1 orange*
6 thick slices of toast, crusts removed	*6 thick slices of toast, crusts removed*
about 50 g butter or margarine	*about 2 oz butter or margarine*
100 g soft brown sugar	*4 oz soft brown sugar*
300 ml milk	*½ pint milk*
2 eggs, lightly beaten	*2 eggs, lightly beaten*
1 × 1.25 ml ground cinnamon	*¼ teaspoon ground cinnamon*

EVERYDAY PUDDINGS

Attempting to provide a different pudding for each day is a challenge to every cook. Desserts for dinner parties and other special occasions can easily be different and exciting, when time and expense are not spared, but everyday puddings must usually be prepared in next to no time, and a watchful eye must be kept on the cost of the ingredients. The recipes in this chapter illustrate how easy it is, with a little care and imagination, to 'dress up' basic everyday ingredients. Recipes which are especially quick and easy to make are denoted by a Q symbol followed by the number of minutes it takes to prepare them (excluding chilling or cooking time).

Pears en chemise

Metric	Imperial
6 large firm cooking pears (Conference type)	6 large firm cooking pears (Conference type)
4 × 15 ml spoons seedless raisins	4 tablespoons seedless raisins
3 × 15 ml spoons soft brown sugar	3 tablespoons soft brown sugar
1 × 1.25 ml spoon ground cinnamon	¼ teaspoon ground cinnamon
2 × 5 ml spoons rum essence (optional)	2 teaspoons rum essence (optional)
1 × 400 g packet frozen puff pastry, thawed	1 × 14 oz packet frozen puff pastry, thawed
½ egg, lightly beaten	½ egg, lightly beaten
2 × 15 ml spoons caster sugar	2 tablespoons caster sugar

Cooking time: 40 to 50 minutes
Oven: 190°C, 375°F, Gas Mark 5

Peel the pears, then core them carefully from the bottom end and trim the bottoms so that the pears will stand upright. Do not remove the stalks.
Mix together the raisins, brown sugar, cinnamon and rum essence (if using), then fill the cavities in the pears with this mixture.
Roll out the pastry on a lightly floured surface, trim the edges, then cut into 6 squares. Stand 1 pear on each square, then fold the dough around the pear to enclose it completely. Use the trimmings of dough to make a 'cap' for each pear. Leave the stalk protruding at the top of each pear.
Stand the pears upright on a damp baking sheet, then brush all over with the beaten egg and sprinkle with the caster sugar. Bake in a preheated oven for 40 to 50 minutes or until the pastry is golden brown and the pears feel soft when pierced with a skewer. Serve warm with cream or thin pouring custard.
Makes 6

Harlequin tart

Metric	Imperial
225 g plain flour	8 oz plain flour
pinch of salt	pinch of salt
50 g butter or margarine	2 oz butter or margarine
50 g lard	2 oz lard
about 3 × 15 ml spoons water	about 3 tablespoons water

Filling:

Metric	Imperial
1½ × 15 ml spoons red jam	1½ tablespoons red jam
1½ × 15 ml spoons apricot jam	1½ tablespoons apricot jam
3 × 15 ml spoons lemon curd	3 tablespoons lemon curd
3 × 15 ml spoons mincemeat	3 tablespoons mincemeat

Cooking time: 35 minutes
Oven: 190°C, 375°F, Gas Mark 5

Children will love this colourful tart with its choice of different fillings. It is not necessary to use exactly the same combination of fillings as suggested here – you may use whatever ingredients you happen to have in the store cupboard. Try to alternate the colours as much as possible to obtain the most eye-catching results and pleasing taste.

To make the pastry: sift the flour and salt into a bowl. Add the butter or margarine and lard in pieces, then rub into the flour with the fingertips until the mixture resembles fine breadcrumbs. Stir in the water gradually and mix to a firm dough.
Roll out the dough on a lightly floured surface and use to line a 23 cm/9 inch pie plate. Trim the edge and reserve the trimmings.
To make the filling: mark 6 sections on the dough with a sharp knife. Spread the jams, lemon curd and mincemeat in the sections, allowing 1½ × 15 ml spoons/1½ tablespoons for each section and alternating the colours.
Cut the reserved trimmings of dough into thin strips, then twist into spiral shapes and place on top of the filling to separate the sections. Brush the ends of the strips with water, then press firmly to seal around the edge of the plate. Flute the edge in an attractive pattern. Bake in a preheated oven for 35 minutes or until the pastry is golden brown. Remove from the oven and leave to stand for 10 minutes, then serve warm with thin pouring custard.
Serves 6

Pears en chemise; Harlequin tart

Apricot mould

Metric
1 sachet (1×15 ml spoon)
  powdered gelatine
2×15 ml spoons lemon juice
2×15 ml spoons water
1×450 g can apricot halves
50 g caster sugar
150 ml whipping or double
  cream
2 egg whites

Imperial
1 sachet (1 tablespoon)
  powdered gelatine
2 tablespoons lemon juice
2 tablespoons water
1×1 lb can apricot halves
2 oz caster sugar
¼ pint whipping or double
  cream
2 egg whites

Sprinkle the gelatine over the lemon juice and water in a small heatproof bowl, then leave until spongy. Stand the bowl in a pan of hot water and heat gently until the gelatine has dissolved, stirring occasionally. Remove from the heat, then leave until cool.

Meanwhile, put the apricots and their juice with the sugar in a liquidizer, reserving 2 apricot halves for decoration. Blend to a smooth purée.

Stir the cooled gelatine liquid into the apricot purée. Whip the cream until thick, then fold into the apricot purée. Beat the egg whites until stiff, then fold into the apricot mixture until evenly blended.

Pour the mixture into a wet 900 ml/1½ pint mould, then chill in the refrigerator for at least 4 hours until set. Unmould on to a serving dish. Cut the reserved apricots into thin slivers, then use to decorate the top. Serve chilled.

Lemon mousse

Metric
finely grated rind and juice
  of 2 lemons
2×5 ml spoons powdered
  gelatine
3 eggs, separated
75 g caster sugar
few slices of crystallized
  lemon, to decorate
  (optional)

Imperial
finely grated rind and juice
  of 2 lemons
2 teaspoons powdered
  gelatine
3 eggs, separated
3 oz caster sugar
few slices of crystallized
  lemon, to decorate
  (optional)

This is a light-textured mousse with a refreshing, tangy bite. When set, it separates out into two layers, with a clear jelly at the bottom and a fluffy light layer on top. If you wish to make it more special for a dinner party or similar occasion, fold in 150 ml/¼ pint lightly whipped cream before the egg whites.

Make the lemon juice up to 150 ml/¼ pint with water. Sprinkle the gelatine over the liquid in a small heatproof bowl, then leave until spongy. Stand the bowl in a pan of hot water and heat gently until the gelatine has dissolved, stirring occasionally. Remove from the heat, then leave until cool.

Put the egg yolks in a bowl with the lemon rind and sugar. Stir well to mix, then gradually stir in the cooled gelatine liquid.

Beat the egg whites until stiff, then fold into the lemon mixture until evenly mixed. Pour into 4 individual glasses or dishes and chill in the refrigerator for at least 4 hours until set. Decorate with lemon slices before serving, if liked.

Serve chilled.

Lemon mousse; Apricot mould

Orange and lemon chiffon pie

Orange and lemon chiffon pie

Metric
175 g digestive biscuits
50 g demerara or soft
 brown sugar
75 g butter or margarine,
 melted

Filling:
finely grated rind and juice
 of 1 lemon
finely grated rind and juice
 of 1 orange
4×15 ml spoons undiluted
 orange squash
50 g caster sugar
2×15 ml spoons cornflour
2 eggs, separated

Imperial
6 oz digestive biscuits
2 oz demerara or soft
 brown sugar
3 oz butter or margarine,
 melted

Filling:
finely grated rind and juice
 of 1 lemon
finely grated rind and juice
 of 1 orange
4 tablespoons undiluted
 orange squash
2 oz caster sugar
2 tablespoons cornflour
2 eggs, separated

Cooking time: 15 minutes
Oven: 200°C, 400°F, Gas Mark 6

This is an American version of our 'Lemon Meringue Pie' in which the beaten egg whites are folded into the custard mixture rather than spread over the top. The light, fluffy filling makes a good contrast with the crisp, crunchy biscuit base.

To make the biscuit crust: crush the biscuits with a rolling pin between 2 sheets of greaseproof paper, then transfer to a bowl. Add the sugar and melted butter or margarine and stir well to mix. Press the mixture into the base and sides of a 20 cm/8 inch flan ring placed on a baking sheet. Chill in the refrigerator for about 30 minutes until firm.
Meanwhile, make the filling: measure the lemon and orange juice and the orange squash and make up to 300 ml/½ pint with water. Mix the sugar and cornflour together, then mix with a little of the juice to make a smooth paste.
Stir the egg yolks into the cornflour paste in a heavy pan. Stir in the remaining juice and the lemon and orange rinds. Heat gently until the mixture becomes thick, stirring constantly with a wooden spoon. Remove from the heat and leave to cool for 5 to 10 minutes, stirring frequently to prevent any lumps forming.
Beat the egg whites until stiff, then fold into the custard mixture until evenly mixed. Spoon into the biscuit crust, then bake in a preheated oven for 15 minutes. Leave to cool in the flan ring, then chill in the refrigerator. Serve chilled.
Serves 4 to 6

Double-decker gooseberry pie

Metric
350 g plain flour
pinch of salt
75 g butter or margarine
75 g lard
1×15 ml spoon caster sugar
1 egg yolk
cold water to mix

Filling:
750 g gooseberries, topped
  and tailed
100 g sugar
finely grated rind of 1 lemon
1×1.25 ml spoon almond
  essence

To glaze:
1×15 ml spoon milk
1×15 ml spoon caster sugar

Imperial
12 oz plain flour
pinch of salt
3 oz butter or margarine
3 oz lard
1 tablespoon caster sugar
1 egg yolk
cold water to mix

Filling:
1½ lb gooseberries, topped
  and tailed
4 oz sugar
finely grated rind of 1 lemon
¼ teaspoon almond
  essence

To glaze:
1 tablespoon milk
1 tablespoon caster sugar

Cooking time: about 45 minutes
Oven: 220°C, 425°F, Gas Mark 7; reduced to
     180°C, 350°F, Gas Mark 4

To make the pastry: sift the flour and salt into a bowl. Add the butter or margarine and lard in pieces, then rub into the flour with the fingertips until the mixture resembles fine breadcrumbs. Stir in the sugar and egg yolk and mix to a soft dough, adding a little water to bind the mixture together if necessary. Form the dough into a ball, sprinkle with flour, then wrap in foil and chill in the refrigerator for about 30 minutes.
Divide the dough into 3. Roll out 1 piece on a lightly floured surface and use to line a 900 ml/1½ pint pie dish and reserve the remaining pastry.
To make the filling: mix together the gooseberries, sugar, lemon rind and almond essence, then put half this mixture in the dish. Roll out another piece of dough, then place on top of the gooseberries. Cover with the remaining gooseberries.
Roll out the remaining dough and use to cover the pie dish. Brush the edge with water and press firmly to seal. Trim and flute the edge and make an air vent in the centre. Brush the top of the pie with the milk, then sprinkle with the sugar.
Bake in a preheated oven for 15 minutes, then reduce the heat and continue baking for a further 30 minutes or until the pastry is golden brown and the gooseberries are tender when pierced with a skewer. Remove from the oven and leave to stand for about 10 minutes, then serve warm with custard or cream.

Traditional Bakewell pudding

Metric
1×225 g packet frozen puff
  pastry, thawed
4×15 ml spoons red jam
1 egg white
150 g caster sugar
4 egg yolks, beaten
150 g butter, melted and
  cooled
50 g ground almonds

Imperial
1×8 oz packet frozen puff
  pastry, thawed
4 tablespoons red jam
1 egg white
5 oz caster sugar
4 egg yolks, beaten
5 oz butter, melted and
  cooled
2 oz ground almonds

Cooking time: 1 hour
Oven: 190°C, 375°F, Gas Mark 5

This deliciously rich pudding is traditionally served warm, but it is equally good left until the following day and served cold. Shortcrust pastry may be used in place of puff pastry if you prefer (see picture).

Roll out the pastry on a lightly floured surface and use to line a greased 23 cm/9 inch flan dish or sandwich tin. Spread the jam over the pastry.
Beat the egg white and sugar together until thick and white, then mix with the egg yolks until well combined. Fold in the melted butter, then the almonds.
Pour into the dish or tin, then bake in a preheated oven for 1 hour or until the filling is set. Cover loosely with foil if the filling becomes too brown during cooking. Leave to stand for 15 minutes, then serve warm.
Serves 6

Double-decker gooseberry pie;
Traditional Bakewell pudding; Pommé

Pommé

Metric	Imperial
4 medium cooking apples	*4 medium cooking apples*
75 g apricot jam	*3 oz apricot jam*
50 g demerara sugar	*2 oz demerara sugar*
1×400 g packet frozen puff pastry, thawed	*1×14 oz packet frozen puff pastry, thawed*
½ egg, lightly beaten	*½ egg, lightly beaten*
1×15 ml spoon caster sugar	*1 tablespoon caster sugar*

Cooking time: 30 to 40 minutes
Oven: 200°C, 400°F, Gas Mark 6

The quantities for this apple cake can easily be halved if you wish to make a smaller dessert, but for the little extra time and trouble involved it is well worth making a larger quantity than required. Pommé is excellent when served cold with cream, or at tea-time.

Peel and core the apples, then cut into very thin, even-sized slices. Put the slices in a bowl with the jam and demerara sugar and fold gently to mix.
Divide the pastry in half, then roll out one half on a lightly floured surface to a 30×20 cm/12×8 inch rectangle. Place the rectangle on a damp baking sheet. Spread the apple mixture evenly over the pastry, leaving a margin around the edge. Brush the margin with water. Roll out the remaining pastry and use to cover the apple mixture, pressing the edges firmly to seal. Trim, knock up and flute the edges, then mark the top of the pastry in a criss-cross pattern and cut an air vent in the centre.
Brush the pastry with the beaten egg and sprinkle with the caster sugar. Bake in a preheated oven for 30 to 40 minutes until the pastry is golden brown and the apples feel tender when pierced with a skewer. Serve hot or cold.
Cuts into 12 squares

Steamed chocolate soufflé

Metric
50 g butter or margarine
150 ml milk
75 g caster sugar
100 g plain chocolate,
    broken into pieces
100 g fresh white
    breadcrumbs
3 eggs, separated

Imperial
2 oz butter or margarine
¼ pint milk
3 oz caster sugar
4 oz plain chocolate,
    broken into pieces
4 oz fresh white
    breadcrumbs
3 eggs, separated

This soufflé is made with breadcrumbs and therefore has a firmer texture than the usual hot soufflé mixture made with flour. If not eaten immediately after steaming, it will shrink away from the sides of the dish and become more dense in texture, but it will still be good to eat.

Put the butter or margarine, milk, sugar and chocolate in a pan and heat gently until the butter and chocolate have melted and the sugar has dissolved, stirring. Remove from the heat, stir in the breadcrumbs, then stir in the egg yolks. Beat the egg whites until stiff, then fold into the mixture until evenly mixed.
Spoon the mixture into a lightly buttered 900 ml/1½ pint soufflé dish, then stand the dish in a pan of gently simmering water. Cover the pan with a lid and steam gently for 2 hours, adding more water as necessary. Serve immediately.
Serves 4 to 6

Old-fashioned rhubarb pudding

Metric
750 g rhubarb, trimmed and
    cut into chunks
finely grated rind and juice
    of 1 orange
150 g demerara sugar
2 × 15 ml spoons golden
    syrup
9 small slices of wholemeal
    bread, crusts removed
100 g butter or margarine,
    softened

Imperial
1½ lb rhubarb, trimmed and
    cut into chunks
finely grated rind and juice
    of 1 orange
5 oz demerara sugar
2 tablespoons golden
    syrup
9 small slices of wholemeal
    bread, crusts removed
4 oz butter or margarine,
    softened

Cooking time: 1 hour
Oven: 190°C, 375°F, Gas Mark 5

Put the rhubarb, orange rind and juice and 100 g/4 oz of the sugar in a heavy pan. Cook for about 5 minutes until the rhubarb is just tender, stirring occasionally. Spread the golden syrup over the inside of a 900 ml/1½ pint ovenproof dish. Spread the bread with the butter or margarine. Put 3 slices of bread, buttered side up, in the bottom of the dish, then cover with half the rhubarb. Put 3 more slices of bread on top, then the remaining rhubarb. Cover with the remaining bread, buttered side down, then press down well.
Cover the dish with foil, then bake in a preheated oven for 1 hour. Remove from the oven, then sprinkle with the remaining sugar and put under a preheated hot grill for 5 to 10 minutes until caramelized. Serve hot with pouring cream or custard.

Steamed chocolate soufflé

Rhubarb and ginger hat; Old-fashioned rhubarb pudding

Rhubarb and ginger hat

Metric
225 g self-raising flour
1 ×1.25 ml spoon salt
100 g shredded suet
about 120 ml water

Imperial
8 oz self-raising flour
¼ teaspoon salt
4 oz shredded suet
about 4 fl oz water

Filling:
450-750 g rhubarb,
  trimmed and cut into
  chunks
100 g demerara sugar
2 ×15 ml spoons ginger
  marmalade
finely grated rind of 1
  orange

Filling:
1-1½ lb rhubarb,
  trimmed and cut into
  chunks
4 oz demerara sugar
2 tablespoons ginger
  marmalade
finely grated rind of 1
  orange

To make the pastry: sift the flour and salt into a bowl. Stir in the suet, then add the water gradually and knead lightly to form a firm dough.
Roll out the dough on a lightly floured surface, then cut out a circle large enough to line the inside of a 900 ml/1½ pint pudding basin. Cut out one-quarter of the circle and roll this out to a smaller circle for the lid. Grease the inside of the basin, then line with the large piece of dough.
To make the filling: put all the ingredients in a bowl and stir well to mix. Spoon into the dough-lined basin, then cover with the reserved dough. Moisten the edges with water and pinch to seal.
Cover the top of the basin with greased foil, making a pleat in the centre to allow the pastry to rise during steaming. Tie securely with string.
Place the basin in the top of a steamer or double boiler, or in a pan half-filled with gently bubbling water. Cover with a lid, then steam for 2 hours, topping up the water level in the pan as necessary.
Remove the foil, then leave the pudding to stand in the basin for 5 minutes. Turn out carefully on to a warmed serving dish. Serve hot with custard.

27

Cheesy orange cream

15

Metric
1 × 600 ml packet orange
jelly
finely grated rind and juice
of 1 orange
1 × 175 g can evaporated
milk, chilled
225 g full-fat soft cheese
few orange slices, to
decorate (optional)

Imperial
1 × 1 pint packet orange
jelly
finely grated rind and juice
of 1 orange
1 × 6 oz can evaporated
milk, chilled
8 oz full-fat soft cheese
few orange slices, to
decorate (optional)

Serve this cool, fruity dessert after a rich main course.

Dissolve the jelly in 150 ml/¼ pint boiling water, then make the liquid up to 450 ml/¾ pint with the orange juice and water. Stir in the orange rind and leave until just beginning to set.

Whip the evaporated milk until thick, then gradually beat into the soft cheese until well combined. Fold the jelly into the cheese mixture until evenly mixed, then pour into a wet 1.2 litre/2 pint mould. Chill in the refrigerator for at least 4 hours until set, then unmould on to a serving dish. Decorate with orange slices, if liked. Serve chilled.

Upside-down fruit pudding

Metric	Imperial
4 × 15 ml spoons golden syrup	4 tablespoons golden syrup
1 × 450 g can fruit (apricot halves, pear halves, pineapple, etc)	1 × 1 lb can fruit (apricot halves, pear halves, pineapple, etc)
about 14 glacé cherries	about 14 glacé cherries
100 g self-raising flour	4 oz self-raising flour
1 × 5 ml spoon baking powder	1 teaspoon baking powder
100 g caster sugar	4 oz caster sugar
100 g soft (tub) margarine	4 oz soft (tub) margarine
2 eggs, lightly beaten	2 eggs, lightly beaten

Cooking time: 50 minutes
Oven: 190°C, 375°F, Gas Mark 5

Spread the golden syrup on the bottom and sides of a lightly buttered 1.2 litre/2 pint ovenproof dish. Arrange the fruit in the bottom of the dish, putting a glacé cherry in the centre of each piece of fruit.
Sift the flour and baking powder into a bowl. Add the remaining ingredients, then beat for 2 to 3 minutes until the mixture is soft and light. Spread the mixture over the fruit.
Bake in a preheated oven for 50 minutes until a skewer inserted in the centre of the pudding comes out clean. Remove from the oven and leave to stand for 5 minutes, then turn out on to a warmed serving dish. Serve hot with custard.
Serves 4 to 6

Individual fruit bumpers

Metric	Imperial
225 g self-raising flour	8 oz self-raising flour
1 × 1.25 ml spoon salt	¼ teaspoon salt
100 g shredded suet	4 oz shredded suet
about 120 ml water	about 4 fl oz water

Filling:	Filling:
2 cooking apples, peeled, cored and grated	2 cooking apples, peeled, cored and grated
2 × 15 ml spoons blackcurrant jam	2 tablespoons blackcurrant jam
50 g caster sugar	2 oz caster sugar

To glaze:	To glaze:
1-2 × 15 ml spoons milk	1-2 tablespoons milk
1 × 15 ml spoon caster sugar	1 tablespoon caster sugar

Cooking time: 30 minutes
Oven: 200°C, 400°F, Gas Mark 6

To make the pastry: sift the flour and salt into a bowl. Stir in the suet, then add the water gradually and knead lightly to form a firm dough. Divide into 8 pieces. Roll out the pieces on a lightly floured surface into thin circles.
To make the filling: put all the ingredients in a bowl and stir well to mix. Divide the filling equally between the circles of dough. Brush the edges of the dough with water, then fold the dough around the filling to enclose it completely. Pinch the edges firmly to seal.
Brush the bumpers with milk, then sprinkle with the sugar. Bake in a preheated oven for 30 minutes until golden brown. Serve hot with custard.

Cheesy orange cream; Upside-down fruit pudding;
Individual fruit bumpers

Pancake parcels

Metric
100 g plain flour
1 × 1.25 ml spoon salt
1 egg
300 ml milk
vegetable oil for frying

Filling:
3 bananas
juice of 1 lemon
2 × 15 ml spoons apricot jam

Sauce:
4 × 15 ml spoons undiluted
    orange squash
2 × 15 ml spoons soft brown
    sugar
25 g butter or margarine
1 × 2.5 ml spoon ground
    cinnamon

Imperial
4 oz plain flour
¼ teaspoon salt
1 egg
½ pint milk
vegetable oil for frying

Filling:
3 bananas
juice of 1 lemon
2 tablespoons apricot jam

Sauce:
4 tablespoons undiluted
    orange squash
2 tablespoons soft brown
    sugar
1 oz butter or margarine
½ teaspoon ground
    cinnamon

To make the batter: sift the flour and salt into a bowl and make a well in the centre. Add the egg, then gradually beat in the milk, drawing in the flour from the sides to make a smooth batter.

Heat a little oil in a frying pan until very hot. Pour in a few spoonfuls of batter, tilting the pan so that it spreads evenly, and cook over high heat until golden brown. Turn over the pancake and cook the underneath until golden brown. Remove from the pan and keep hot while frying the remaining batter, making 8 pancakes in all.

To make the filling: peel the bananas, then mash the flesh with the lemon juice and jam. Divide the filling equally between the pancakes, then fold each pancake around the filling to make a 'parcel'.

To make the sauce: make the orange squash up to 150 ml/¼ pint with water, then pour into a large frying pan. Add the remaining ingredients and bring to the boil, stirring constantly. Boil for 5 minutes until reduced, then lower the heat. Arrange the pancake parcels in a single layer in the pan, then heat through for about 10 minutes, spooning the sauce over the pancakes from time to time. Serve hot, with cream.

North country apple pie

North country apple pie

Metric	Imperial
275 g plain flour	*10 oz plain flour*
pinch of salt	*pinch of salt*
65 g butter or margarine	*2½ oz butter or margarine*
65 g lard	*2½ oz lard*
3-4 ×15 ml spoons water	*3-4 tablespoons water*
1 egg white, lightly beaten	*1 egg white, lightly beaten*

Filling:	Filling:
3 large cooking apples	*3 large cooking apples*
juice of 1 lemon	*juice of 1 lemon*
500-100 g Lancashire	*2-4 oz Lancashire*
cheese, crumbled	*cheese, crumbled*
75 g demerara sugar	*3 oz demerara sugar*
1 ×1.25 ml spoon ground	*¼ teaspoon ground*
mixed spice	*mixed spice*

Left: Pancake parcels

Cooking time: about 45 minutes
Oven: 220°C, 425°F, Gas Mark 7; reduced to
 180°C, 350°F, Gas Mark 4

To make the pastry: sift the flour and salt into a bowl. Add the butter or margarine and lard in pieces, then rub into the flour with the fingertips until the mixture resembles fine breadcrumbs. Stir in the water gradually and mix to a firm dough.
Divide the dough in half, then roll out one half on a lightly floured surface and use to line a 23 cm/9 inch pie plate. Brush with a little beaten egg white.
To make the filling: peel and core the apples, then slice as thinly as possible. Sprinkle with the lemon juice to prevent discolouration. Put half the apple slices on the dough, then sprinkle with half the cheese, sugar and mixed spice. Repeat these layers once more, reserving a little sugar for the top of the pie. Brush the edge of the dough with a little egg white. Roll out the remaining dough and use to cover the pie. Press the edge firmly to seal, trim and flute, then cut an air vent in the centre of the pie. Brush with the remaining egg white, then sprinkle with the reserved sugar.
Bake in a preheated oven for 15 minutes, then lower the heat and continue baking for a further 30 minutes or until the pastry is golden brown and the apples are tender when pierced with a skewer. Remove from the oven and leave to stand for about 10 minutes, then serve warm with custard or cream.
Serves 6

Mock cream

10

Metric
150 ml milk
100 g unsalted butter
1 × 2.5 ml spoon powdered
  gelatine

Imperial
¼ pint milk
4 oz unsalted butter
½ teaspoon powdered
  gelatine

Mock cream makes a good standby for fresh cream. It is made from simple ingredients which are usually to hand, and costs considerably less than double cream. It makes an excellent substitute for double cream when used in mousses and other similar desserts.

Put the milk in a pan, add the butter in pieces and heat gently until the butter has melted.
Remove the milk from the heat, sprinkle over the gelatine and stir well to mix. Leave to cool for 1 to 2 minutes, transfer to an electric blender and blend for 2 minutes until creamy. Chill in the refrigerator, then whip as required.
Makes 300 ml/½ pint

Rich rice meringue

Metric	Imperial
3×15 ml spoons short-grain rice	3 tablespoons short-grain rice
600 ml milk	1 pint milk
25 g butter or margarine	1 oz butter or margarine
1 cinnamon stick	1 cinnamon stick
75 g caster sugar	3 oz caster sugar
2 eggs, separated	2 eggs, separated

Cooking time: 30 minutes
Oven: 190°C, 375°F, Gas Mark 5

Put the rice in a pan with the milk, butter or margarine, cinnamon stick and 25 g/1 oz of the sugar. Bring to the boil, stir once, then lower the heat. Cover with a tight-fitting lid and simmer gently for about 1 hour or until the rice is tender and has absorbed most of the milk. Stir the rice occasionally during cooking to prevent sticking. Remove from the heat, then leave to cool for 15 minutes.
Discard the cinnamon stick. Stir the egg yolks into the rice mixture, then pour into a lightly buttered oven-proof dish. Beat the egg whites until stiff, then fold in the remaining sugar and continue beating until glossy. Spread or pipe the meringue mixture over the top of the pudding. Bake in a preheated oven for 30 minutes until lightly browned and crisp.
Serve hot.

Apple beignets

Metric	Imperial
225 g plain flour	8 oz plain flour
75 ml vegetable oil	3 fl oz vegetable oil
300 ml cider	½ pint cider
1 egg white	1 egg white
vegetable oil for deep-frying	vegetable oil for deep-frying
4 large cooking apples	4 large cooking apples
juice of 1 lemon	juice of 1 lemon

To finish:	To finish:
about 75 g caster sugar	about 3 oz caster sugar
1×2.5 ml spoon ground cinnamon	½ teaspoon ground cinnamon

The addition of beaten egg white makes this batter particularly light, but it must be used as soon as the egg white is incorporated or it will collapse.

To make the batter: sift the flour into a bowl, make a well in the centre, then stir in the oil, gradually drawing in the flour from the sides of the bowl. Add the cider gradually, beating with a whisk to make a smooth batter.
Heat the oil in a deep-fat fryer to 190°C/375°F. Meanwhile, peel and core the apples, then slice into rings. Sprinkle the rings with the lemon juice to prevent discolouration.
Beat the egg white until stiff, then fold into the batter until evenly mixed. Dip the apple rings in the batter until well coated, then deep-fry a few at a time in the hot oil for a few minutes until golden on both sides. Drain on absorbent kitchen paper. Mix together the sugar and cinnamon, then sprinkle over the beignets. Serve immediately.

Apple beignets; Rich rice meringue; Mock cream

Traditional baked cheesecake

Traditional baked cheesecake

Cooking time: 1 hour
Oven: 180°C, 350°F, Gas Mark 4

This cheesecake is good served with morning coffee or afternoon tea, as an alternative to the more usual cakes and pastries.

Metric
175 g plain flour
pinch of salt
40 g butter or margarine
40 g lard
about 2×15 ml spoons
   water
½ egg white, stirred

Filling:
50 g butter or margarine
50 g caster sugar
450 g curd cheese
2 grade 1 or 2 eggs, beaten
100 g seedless raisins
25 g ground almonds
finely grated rind and juice
   of 1 lemon
25 g demerara sugar

Imperial
6 oz plain flour
pinch of salt
1½ oz butter or margarine
1½ oz lard
about 2 tablespoons
   water
½ egg white, stirred

Filling:
2 oz butter or margarine
2 oz caster sugar
1 lb curd cheese
2 grade 1 or 2 eggs, beaten
4 oz seedless raisins
1 oz ground almonds
finely grated rind and juice
   of 1 lemon
1 oz demerara sugar

To make the pastry: sift the flour and salt into a bowl. Add the butter or margarine and lard in pieces, then rub into the flour with the fingertips until the mixture resembles fine breadcrumbs. Stir in the water gradually and mix to a firm dough.
Roll out the dough on a lightly floured surface and use it to line an 18 cm/7 inch loose-bottomed springform pan. Trim and flute the edge, then brush all over the dough with the egg white. Chill in the refrigerator while preparing the filling.
To make the filling: put the butter or margarine and sugar in a bowl and cream together until light and fluffy. Add the curd cheese and continue beating until soft, then beat in the remaining ingredients one at a time, except the demerara sugar.
Spoon the filling into the pastry lined pan, then sprinkle with the demerara sugar. Stand the pan on a baking sheet, then bake in the oven for 50 minutes or until the filling is set. Remove the pan carefully from the sides of the cheesecake and return to the oven for a further 10 minutes until the pastry is golden. Remove from the oven and leave until cold, then place on a serving platter and cut into slices. Serve cold.
Serves 8

Chilled mandarin cheesecake

Metric
175 g digestive biscuits
50 g shelled hazelnuts or
 walnuts, finely chopped
100 g butter, melted
1×350 g can mandarins
1 sachet (1×15 ml spoon)
 powdered gelatine
finely grated rind and juice
 of 1 lemon
350 g full-fat soft cheese
150 ml soured cream
75 g caster sugar
2 eggs, separated

Imperial
6 oz digestive biscuits
2 oz shelled hazelnuts or
 walnuts, finely chopped
4 oz butter, melted
1×12 oz can mandarins
1 sachet (1 tablespoon)
 powdered gelatine
finely grated rind and juice
 of 1 lemon
12 oz full-fat soft cheese
¼ pint soured cream
3 oz caster sugar
2 eggs, separated

Crush the biscuits in an electric blender or between 2 sheets of greaseproof paper. Mix them with the chopped nuts and melted butter, then press into the base of a buttered loose-bottomed 20 cm/8 inch springform pan. Chill in the refrigerator for about 30 minutes until firm.

Meanwhile, drain and reserve the mandarins and measure 150 ml/¼ pint juice. Sprinkle the gelatine over the juice in a small heatproof bowl, then leave until spongy. Stand the bowl in a pan of hot water and heat gently until the gelatine has dissolved, stirring occasionally. Remove from the heat, stir in the lemon rind and juice, then leave until cold.

Put the cheese, soured cream and sugar in a bowl and beat together until soft, then stir in the egg yolks until evenly blended. Stir in the cooled gelatine liquid.

Beat the egg whites until stiff, then fold into the cream cheese mixture. Pour into the biscuit lined pan, then chill in the refrigerator overnight until set. Remove the cheesecake from the pan, place on a serving platter and decorate with the reserved mandarin oranges. Serve chilled.

Serves 8

Chilled mandarin cheesecake

ICED DESSERTS

Now that refrigerators and freezers are commonplace items of kitchen equipment, homemade iced desserts have really come into their own. Gone is the arduous task of operating an unwieldy ice cream churn by hand, for nowadays electric equipment helps to make perfect ices at home, with little or no extra effort on your part! Obviously you will feel more inclined to experiment with ice cream during the hot summer weather, but don't neglect these desserts in the depths of winter, when they can make a refreshing end to rich dinner party meals.

Some helpful hints:
Ice creams, water ices and sorbets can be made in the freezing compartment of a refrigerator with a 3 star marking, or in a domestic freezer. If you intend to make ices regularly, an electric ice cream churn is a worthwhile buy because it gives the finished ice a much smoother texture than it is possible to achieve by hand beating.

If you do not have an ice cream churn, however, the following rules will help to give good results when making the iced desserts in this chapter.

1. If using the freezing compartment of a refrigerator, turn the temperature control down to its coldest setting at least 1 hour before making ice cream, and make room on the floor of the freezing compartment for the ice cream container. If using a freezer, make room on the floor or in the coldest part of the freezer.

2. Try to work in the coolest part of the kitchen and chill all bowls, containers and utensils before using them. Metal containers are best for fast freezing, therefore these should be used if possible.

3. Always chill mixtures in the refrigerator before freezing. Allow at least 30 minutes for this chilling – it helps the mixture freeze faster and thus prevents ice crystals forming.

4. When the mixture begins to harden around the edges and becomes slushy (the length of time this takes varies according to individual recipes, but is usually a minimum of 45 minutes), remove from the freezing compartment or freezer. Beat vigorously to break down the ice crystals, using a rotary or electric beater, or by working the mixture in an electric blender. Return the mixture to the freezer and freeze again. If liked, the mixture can be beaten again when slushy to break down more ice crystals, however this is not absolutely necessary and the ice cream can be left to become firm at this stage. The more ice cream you make, the more you will be able to judge just how often the mixture needs beating – some mixtures need far more beating than others.

5. Allow the mixture to mature and ripen before serving. This will take at least 2 hours after the mixture has become firm, depending on the individual recipe. Most iced desserts benefit from being left overnight.

6. Allow the mixture to soften slightly before serving or it will be tasteless and too hard to eat. Stand ice creams in the main body of the refrigerator for about 30 minutes, water ices and sorbets at room temperature for 10 to 20 minutes. These times can only be a rough guide, however, as they will obviously vary according to the type of mixture, size of container and the temperature of the room or refrigerator.

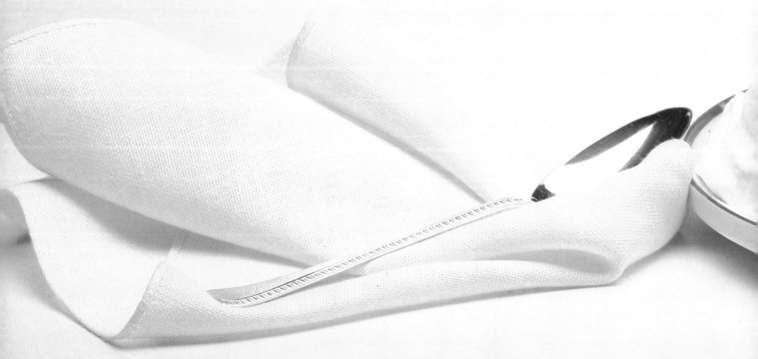

Strawberry baked Alaska

Metric
about 350 g fresh
  strawberries, hulled and
  sliced
4-6×15 ml spoons Marsala
  or sweet sherry
3 egg whites
100 g caster sugar
1×20 cm sponge flan case
450 ml Rich Vanilla
  Ice Cream (page 41)

Imperial
about ¾ lb fresh
  strawberries, hulled and
  sliced
4-6 tablespoons Marsala
  or sweet sherry
3 egg whites
4 oz caster sugar
1×8 inch sponge flan case
¾ pint Rich Vanilla Ice
  Cream (page 41)

Cooking time: 3 minutes
Oven: 230°C, 450°F, Gas Mark 8

Baked Alaska always makes an impressive dinner party dessert, but it does have to be prepared at the last minute or the ice cream will melt. To make things easier, a version without the strawberries can be made in advance and frozen until solid. Follow the recipe up until baking, then freeze the dessert. To serve, bake from frozen for about 5 minutes until thawed.

Put the strawberries in a bowl, sprinkle over half the Marsala or sherry, then leave to macerate.
Meanwhile, beat the egg whites until stiff, fold in the sugar, then beat again until glossy. Set aside. Stand the flan case on a heatproof serving platter and sprinkle over the remaining Marsala or sherry.
Pile the macerated strawberries in the flan case. Soften the ice cream slightly, then spread it over the strawberries in a dome shape. Spoon the meringue mixture quickly over the ice cream and flan case to cover them completely, then bake immediately in the oven for about 3 minutes until the meringue is lightly browned. Serve immediately.
Serves 6

Strawberry baked Alaska

Minted chocolate ice cream

Metric	Imperial
100 g plain chocolate	4 oz plain chocolate
2×15 ml spoons milk	2 tablespoons milk
1×5 ml spoon peppermint essence	1 teaspoon peppermint essence
1 egg	1 egg
1 egg yolk	1 egg yolk
75 g caster sugar	3 oz caster sugar
150 ml double or whipping cream	¼ pint double or whipping cream
150 ml single cream	¼ pint single cream

This is a luxuriously rich and creamy ice that is best reserved for dinner parties and other very special occasions.

If using the refrigerator, turn it to its coldest setting.

Put the chocolate, milk and peppermint essence in a heatproof bowl standing over a pan of gently bubbling water and heat gently until the chocolate has melted, stirring occasionally. Remove from the heat and leave to cool.
Meanwhile, put the egg, egg yolk and sugar in a separate heatproof bowl and stand over the pan of water. Whisk with a rotary beater or balloon whisk until the mixture is thick and creamy and the beater leaves a ribbon trail behind it when lifted. Remove the bowl from the heat and continue whisking until the mixture is cold.
Stir the egg mixture into the cooled chocolate until evenly blended. Whip the creams together until they just hold their shape, then fold them into the chocolate mixture. Pour into a freezing container, then chill in the refrigerator for at least 30 minutes. Transfer to the freezing compartment of the refrigerator or to the freezer and freeze for about 45 minutes or until slushy.
Remove the ice cream and beat thoroughly, then return to the freezing compartment or freezer and freeze overnight or until required. Serve straight from the freezer.
Return the refrigerator to its normal setting.
Keeps for 1 to 2 months

Variation:
For a plain chocolate-flavoured ice cream, omit the peppermint essence.

Cassata Siciliana

Metric	Imperial
600 ml vanilla ice cream	1 pint vanilla ice cream
450 ml chocolate ice cream	¾ pint chocolate ice cream
150 ml double or whipping cream	¼ pint double or whipping cream
50 g icing sugar	2 oz icing sugar
100 g candied fruits, finely chopped	4 oz candied fruits, finely chopped

If using the refrigerator, turn it to its coldest setting.

Soften three-quarters of the vanilla ice cream slightly, then use it to line the inside of a 1 litre/2 pint mould, pudding basin or foil container. Put in the freezing compartment of the refrigerator or in the freezer and freeze until solid.
Soften the chocolate ice cream slightly, then use to make a layer inside the vanilla ice cream, leaving a well in the centre. Freeze until solid.
Whip the cream until it just holds its shape, then add the icing sugar and continue whipping until thick. Fold in the fruits, then spoon the mixture into the well in the centre of the cassata. Freeze until solid.
Soften the remaining vanilla ice cream slightly, then spread over the top of the cream to cover it completely. Cover the mould with a lid or foil, then freeze until required.
To serve: dip the mould in hot water for 1 to 2 seconds, then unmould the cassata on to a chilled serving platter. Serve immediately.
Return the refrigerator to its normal setting.
Keeps for 1 to 2 months
Serves 6 to 8

Cassata Siciliana; Minted chocolate ice cream

Rich vanilla ice cream; Quick fruit ice cream; Coffee and hazelnut ice cream

Coffee and hazelnut ice cream

Metric
1×15 ml spoon instant
  coffee powder or granules
1×15 ml spoon hot water
300 ml double or whipping
  cream
150 ml single cream
75 g icing sugar
50 g shelled hazelnuts,
  finely chopped

Imperial
1 tablespoon instant
  coffee powder or granules
1 tablespoon hot water
½ pint double or whipping
  cream
¼ pint single cream
3 oz icing sugar
2 oz shelled hazelnuts,
  finely chopped

This deliciously rich and creamy ice cream is very simple to make.

If using the refrigerator, turn it to its coldest setting.

Dissolve the coffee in the hot water, then leave to cool. Whip the creams together until they just hold their shape. Add the icing sugar and whip again, then stir in the cool coffee liquid and the hazelnuts.

Pour the mixture into a freezer container, then chill in the refrigerator for at least 30 minutes. Transfer to the freezing compartment of the refrigerator or to the freezer and freeze for about 45 minutes or until slushy. Remove and beat thoroughly, then cover and freeze again for at least 2 hours or until firm.

To serve: transfer the ice cream to the main body of the refrigerator for about 30 minutes to soften slightly, then scoop into individual glasses or bowls. Serve immediately.

Return the refrigerator to its normal setting.

Keeps for 1 to 2 months

Rich vanilla ice cream

Metric	Imperial
300 ml single cream	½ pint single cream
1 vanilla pod	1 vanilla pod
4 egg yolks	4 egg yolks
50 g caster sugar	2 oz caster sugar
300 ml double or whipping cream	½ pint double or whipping cream

This kind of ice cream made with a rich egg custard base is best made in an ice cream churn for the smoothest results. To do this, fold the whipped double cream into the cooled custard mixture, then chill it in the refrigerator for at least 30 minutes. Pour the mixture into the ice cream churn and freeze according to the manufacturer's instructions.

If using the refrigerator, turn it to its coldest setting.

Put the single cream and vanilla pod in a heavy pan and bring slowly to just below boiling point. Remove from the heat and leave to infuse.
Meanwhile, put the egg yolks and sugar in a heatproof bowl standing over a pan of gently bubbling water. Stir with a wooden spoon until thick and creamy, then gradually stir in the scalded cream, discarding the vanilla pod. Continue stirring for about 15 minutes until the custard is thick enough to coat the back of the spoon, then remove from the heat and leave to cool.
Pour the cooled mixture into a freezer container, then transfer to the freezing compartment of the refrigerator or to the freezer for about 45 minutes or until slushy. Whip the double or whipping cream until it just holds its shape. Remove the slushy cream mixture from the freezing compartment or freezer, beat thoroughly, then fold in the cream until evenly blended. Return the mixture to the container, cover and freeze for a further 45 minutes, then beat again until smooth.
Freeze the ice cream for at least 1 to 2 hours or until required, then transfer to the main part of the refrigerator for about 15 minutes to soften slightly before serving in individual glasses or bowls.
Return the refrigerator to its normal setting.
Keeps for 1 to 2 months
Serves 6

Quick fruit ice cream

Metric	Imperial
1×175 g can evaporated milk	1×6 oz can evaporated milk
1×450 g can raspberries	1×1 lb can raspberries
2 egg whites	2 egg whites
50 g caster sugar	2 oz caster sugar

Canned strawberries, loganberries or apricots can be used instead of the raspberries suggested here.

If using the refrigerator, turn it to its coldest setting.

Put the can of evaporated milk in a pan of boiling water and boil for 15 minutes. Leave to cool, then chill in the refrigerator for about 1 hour or until very cold.
Meanwhile, rub the raspberries and their juice through a sieve and measure 300 ml/½ pint purée, making the volume up with water if necessary.
Whip the evaporated milk until thick, then fold in the raspberry purée until evenly blended. Beat the egg whites and sugar together until stiff, then fold them into the raspberry mixture. Pour into a freezer container and chill in the refrigerator for at least 30 minutes, then transfer to the freezing compartment of the refrigerator or to the freezer and freeze for about 45 minutes or until slushy.
Remove the mixture from the freezing compartment or freezer, beat thoroughly, then return to the container. Cover and freeze for at least 2 hours or until required. Stand the ice cream at room temperature for about 10 minutes to soften slightly, then scoop into individual glasses or bowls.
Serve immediately.
Return the refrigerator to its normal setting.
Keeps for 1 to 2 months
Serves 6

Kulfi (Indian almond ice cream)

Metric	Imperial
600 ml milk	1 pint milk
2 eggs	2 eggs
2 egg yolks	2 egg yolks
100 g caster sugar	4 oz caster sugar
50 g ground almonds	2 oz ground almonds
1×1.25 ml spoon almond essence	¼ teaspoon almond essence
1×15 ml spoon rose water (optional)	1 tablespoon rose water (optional)
300 ml double or whipping cream	½ pint double or whipping cream

To serve:	To serve:
25-50 g blanched almonds or pistachio nuts, finely chopped	1-2 oz blanched almonds or pistachio nuts, finely chopped

This is an adaptation of a traditional Indian recipe called Kulfi. It is very rich and creamy and would make an ideal dinner party dessert, particularly after a main course of curry.

If using the refrigerator, turn it to its coldest setting.

Put the milk in a pan and bring slowly to boiling point. Put the eggs, egg yolks and caster sugar in a heatproof bowl and whisk together until evenly blended. Add the scalded milk gradually, stirring constantly, then stand the bowl over a pan of gently bubbling water and continue stirring until the custard thickens and just coats the back of the spoon. Remove from the heat and leave to cool.
Stir in the ground almonds, almond essence and rose water (if using), then pour the mixture into a freezer container and chill in the refrigerator for at least 30 minutes. Transfer to the freezing compartment of the refrigerator or to the freezer and freeze for about 45 minutes or until slushy, then remove and beat thoroughly.
Whip the cream until it just holds its shape, then fold it into the beaten custard until evenly blended. Return the mixture to the freezing compartment or freezer and freeze for a further 45 minutes or until slushy. Remove and beat thoroughly, then cover the container and freeze until firm, preferably overnight to allow the ice cream to mature.
To serve: transfer the ice cream to the main body of the refrigerator for about 30 minutes to soften slightly, then scoop into individual glasses or bowls and sprinkle with the chopped nuts. Serve immediately.
Return the refrigerator to its normal setting.
Keeps for 1 to 2 months
Serves 6 to 8

Fresh pineapple water ice

Metric	Imperial
450 ml water	¾ pint water
150 g granulated sugar	5 oz granulated sugar
1 strip of lemon rind	1 strip of lemon rind
1 fresh ripe pineapple (about 1¼ kg)	1 fresh ripe pineapple (about 2½ lb)
2×5 ml spoons powdered gelatine	2 teaspoons powdered gelatine

If using the refrigerator, turn it to its coldest setting.

Put the water, sugar and lemon rind in a heavy pan and heat gently until the sugar has dissolved. Bring to the boil, then boil for 5 minutes until syrupy. Remove from the heat, leave to cool, then remove and discard the lemon rind.
Meanwhile, cut the pineapple in half lengthways and scoop out the flesh. Reserve the shells, wrap closely in foil and chill in the refrigerator until serving time. Purée the flesh in an electric blender and measure 450 ml/¾ pint of it.
Sprinkle the gelatine over 150 ml/¼ pint of the cooled syrup in a small bowl, stir to dissolve then leave for 5 minutes. Stand the bowl in a pan of hot water and heat gently until dissolved. Stir it into the remaining syrup, then leave until completely cold.
Combine the syrup and pineapple purée, then pour into a freezer container and chill in the refrigerator for at least 30 minutes. Transfer to the freezing compartment of the refrigerator or to the freezer and freeze for 1 to 2 hours or until slushy.
Remove the mixture from the freezing compartment or freezer, beat thoroughly, then return to the container. Cover and freeze for at least 2 hours or until firm. Stand the water ice at room temperature for 10 to 20 minutes to soften slightly, then scoop into the chilled pineapple shells. Serve immediately.
Return the refrigerator to its normal setting.
Keeps for 2 months
Serves 4 to 6

Fresh pineapple water ice; Kulfi (Indian almond ice cream)

Knickerbocker glory

Metric
1 ×600 ml packet raspberry
  jelly

Melba sauce:
1 ×225 g can raspberries
juice of ½ lemon
50 g caster sugar
2 ×5 ml spoons arrowroot
2 large ripe peaches, stoned
  and sliced
2 bananas
450 ml Rich Vanilla Ice
  Cream (page 41)
50 g shelled hazelnuts,
  finely chopped
150 ml whipping cream,
  stiffly whipped
4 cherries (fresh or glacé)

Imperial
1 ×1 pint packet raspberry
  jelly

Melba sauce:
1 ×8 oz can raspberries
juice of ½ lemon
2 oz caster sugar
2 teaspoons arrowroot
2 large ripe peaches, stoned
  and sliced
2 bananas
¾ pint Rich Vanilla Ice
  Cream (page 41)
2 oz shelled hazelnuts,
  finely chopped
¼ pint whipping cream,
  stiffly whipped
4 cherries (fresh or glacé)

Make the jelly according to packet directions, then
leave to set.

Meanwhile, make the Melba sauce: put the raspberries, lemon juice and sugar in a pan and heat gently
until the sugar has dissolved. Remove from the heat,
then rub through a sieve into a measuring jug.
Measure 150 ml/¼ pint purée, making it up with water
as necessary. Mix the arrowroot to a paste with a little
cold water. Return the purée to the rinsed-out pan, stir
in the arrowroot paste and bring to the boil. Lower the
heat and simmer until the sauce thickens, stirring
constantly. Leave until cool.
Chop the jelly roughly, then put 1 spoonful in the
bottom of each of 4 Knickerbocker Glory or sundae
glasses. Put a few peach slices on top of the jelly. Peel
and slice the bananas, then put a few slices on top of
the peaches. Put 1 scoop of ice cream in each glass,
then pour over a little of the Melba sauce and sprinkle
with nuts. Continue with these layers until all the
ingredients are used up, then pipe a whirl of cream on
top of each glass and top with a cherry.
Serve immediately.

Blackcurrant sorbet; Knickerbocker glory; Coffee granita

Coffee granita

Metric	Imperial
4 × 15 ml spoons Continental or other strong blend of freshly ground coffee	4 tablespoons Continental or other strong blend of freshly ground coffee
100 g caster sugar	4 oz caster sugar
450 ml boiling water	¾ pint boiling water

Granita is an Italian water ice which is usually served with whipped cream as a dinner party dessert. It can be made with fruit or coffee and is always served ice cold. Granita is not beaten during freezing and so its texture is coarse and granular – quite different from other water ices and sorbets which have the ice crystals beaten out of them during freezing.

If using the refrigerator, turn it to its coldest setting.

Put the coffee and sugar in a jug and stir in the boiling water. Stir until the coffee and sugar have dissolved, then leave to cool.
Strain the coffee liquid into a freezer container and chill in the refrigerator for at least 30 minutes. Transfer to the freezing compartment of the refrigerator or to the freezer and freeze for at least 2 hours or until completely solid.
Remove the granita from the container, then quickly chop into large chunks with a large strong knife. Return it to the container and freeze again until required. Serve straight from the freezer with whipped cream if liked.
Return the refrigerator to its normal setting.
Keeps for 2 months

Blackcurrant sorbet

Metric	Imperial
300 ml water	½ pint water
175 g granulated sugar	6 oz granulated sugar
juice of ½ lemon	juice of ½ lemon
450 g fresh or frozen blackcurrants	1 lb fresh or frozen blackcurrants
2 egg whites	2 egg whites

If using the refrigerator, turn it to its coldest setting.

Put the water and sugar in a heavy pan and heat gently until the sugar has dissolved. Bring to the boil, then boil for 5 minutes until syrupy. Remove from the heat, stir in the lemon juice, then leave to cool.
Meanwhile, put the blackcurrants in a heavy pan and heat gently for 5 to 10 minutes until the blackcurrants are soft and the juices run. Remove from the heat and push the blackcurrants through a sieve. Leave to cool. Combine the syrup and blackcurrant purée, pour into a freezer container, then chill in the refrigerator for at least 30 minutes. Transfer to the freezing compartment of the refrigerator or to the freezer, then freeze for 1 to 2 hours or until slushy.
Beat the egg whites until stiff. Remove the slushy blackcurrant mixture from the freezing compartment or freezer, beat thoroughly, then fold in the egg whites until evenly blended. Return to the container, cover and freeze for at least 2 hours or until firm. Stand the sorbet at room temperature for 10 to 20 minutes to soften slightly, then scoop into individual glasses or bowls. Serve immediately.
Return the refrigerator to its normal setting.
Keeps for 2 months
Serves 4 to 6

DINNER PARTY DESSERTS

Every ambitious and adventurous cook enjoys the opportunity to demonstrate her culinary skills. The dessert course of a dinner party is one of the occasions when you can do this, especially if plenty of time is set aside beforehand for preparation. For maximum effect, dinner party desserts must look as good as they taste, so take extra care with the finishing touches – piping and decorating are very important. Attention must also be paid to achieving the correct balance between the dessert course and the previous courses in the meal.

Profiteroles with banana cream

Metric
150 ml water
50 g butter or margarine
65 g plain flour, sifted
  with a pinch of salt
2 eggs, beaten

Chocolate sauce:
100 g plain chocolate,
  broken into pieces
2×15 ml spoons brandy or
  water
50 g icing sugar, sifted
25 g unsalted butter

Filling:
300 ml double cream
1 banana
25 g icing sugar, sifted

Imperial
¼ pint water
2 oz butter or margarine
2½ oz plain flour, sifted
  with a pinch of salt
2 eggs, beaten

Chocolate sauce:
4 oz plain chocolate,
  broken into pieces
2 tablespoons brandy or
  water
2 oz icing sugar, sifted
1 oz unsalted butter

Filling:
½ pint double cream
1 banana
1 oz icing sugar, sifted

Cooking time: 15 to 20 minutes
Oven: 220°C, 425°F, Gas Mark 7

The profiteroles can be made 1 to 2 days before required and stored in an airtight tin. They will need 'refreshing' before filling with the banana cream, however, and this should be done by standing the profiteroles on a baking sheet in a preheated oven (180°C, 350°F, Gas Mark 4) for about 5 minutes. Leave to cool on a wire rack before filling.

Put the water in a pan with the butter or margarine and heat gently until the fat has melted. Bring to the boil and, when bubbling vigorously, remove from the heat and immediately add the flour all at once. Beat quickly with a wooden spoon until the mixture forms a ball and draws away from the sides of the pan.
Leave the mixture to cool slightly, then beat in the eggs a little at a time until the pastry is smooth and glossy. Put the mixture in a piping bag fitted with a 1.25 cm/½ inch plain nozzle and pipe about 24 small rounds of pastry on lightly greased baking sheets. Space the rounds well apart to allow for expansion during cooking. Bake just above the centre of a preheated oven for 15 to 20 minutes.
Meanwhile, make the chocolate sauce: put all the ingredients in a heatproof bowl standing over a pan of gently simmering water. Heat gently until all the ingredients are melted and a smooth sauce is formed, stirring with a wooden spoon. Remove from the heat, pour into a serving jug and leave to cool.
When the profiteroles are well risen and golden brown, remove from the baking sheets. Make a slit in the side of each profiterole, then leave them to cool on a wire rack.
Meanwhile, make the filling: whip the cream until it holds its shape. Peel the banana, mash with the icing sugar, then fold into the whipped cream.
To serve: put the banana cream in a piping bag fitted with a small nozzle, then pipe into the profiteroles through the slits in the sides. Pile the profiteroles up on a serving plate, then pour over the chocolate sauce just before serving. Serve immediately.

Profiteroles with banana cream

Chocolate and orange mousse

Metric
175 g plain chocolate,
  broken into pieces
juice of 1 large orange
4 eggs, separated

To decorate:
150 ml double or whipping
  cream
finely grated rind of 1
  orange
2×5 ml spoons orange juice
25-50 g plain chocolate,
  grated

Imperial
6 oz plain chocolate, broken
  into pieces
juice of 1 large orange
4 eggs, separated

To decorate:
¼ pint double or whipping
  cream
finely grated rind of 1
  orange
2 teaspoons orange juice
1-2 oz plain chocolate,
  grated

If you happen to have Grand Marnier in the house, then 4×15 ml/4 tablespoons of this may be substituted for the orange juice.

Put the chocolate and orange juice in a heatproof bowl standing over a pan of gently simmering water. Heat gently until the chocolate has melted, stirring occasionally with a wooden spoon.
Remove the bowl from the heat, leave to cool slightly, then gradually stir in the egg yolks. Leave until cold, stirring occasionally.
Beat the egg whites until stiff, then fold into the egg yolk mixture until evenly blended. Spoon the mousse into 4 individual glasses or dishes, then chill in the refrigerator for at least 4 hours or until firm.
To decorate: put the cream, orange rind and juice in a bowl and whip together until the cream holds its shape. Pipe 1 rosette of cream on top of each mousse, then sprinkle with grated chocolate. Serve chilled.

Chocolate hazelnut gâteau; Chocolate and orange mousse

Chocolate hazelnut gâteau

Metric
100 g self-raising flour
pinch of salt
225 g unsalted butter,
  softened
225 g light soft brown sugar
4 eggs, separated
100 g shelled hazelnuts,
  finely ground
225 g plain chocolate,
  grated

To finish:
300 ml double or whipping
  cream
50 g shelled hazelnuts,
  roughly chopped
175 g plain chocolate,
  broken into pieces
100 g icing sugar, sifted
4 × 15 ml spoons water

Imperial
4 oz self-raising flour
pinch of salt
8 oz unsalted butter,
  softened
8 oz light soft brown sugar
4 eggs, separated
4 oz shelled hazelnuts,
  finely ground
8 oz plain chocolate,
  grated

To finish:
½ pint double or whipping
  cream
2 oz shelled hazelnuts,
  roughly chopped
6 oz plain chocolate, broken
  into pieces
4 oz icing sugar, sifted
4 tablespoons water

Cooking time: 1 hour 15 minutes
Oven: 170°C, 325°F, Gas Mark 3

This cake can be made ahead of time, then stored in an airtight tin for a few days before required. It should not be assembled with the cream and frosting until just before serving, however, as the cream will not keep. For a cake that is less rich, the cream may be omitted and the cake simply served plain with the frosting and nuts on top – this would be more suitable for a tea-time cake rather than a dinner party dessert.

Line the bottom of a greased 23 cm/9 inch deep cake tin with non-stick parchment paper. Sift together the flour and salt and set aside.
Put the butter and sugar in a bowl and beat together until light and fluffy. Beat in the egg yolks one at a time, adding a little of the flour after each addition. Fold in the remaining flour, then the hazelnuts and chocolate. Stir until evenly blended.
Beat the egg whites until stiff, then fold into the cake mixture. Spoon into the prepared tin and level the top. Bake in a preheated oven for 1 hour 15 minutes or until a skewer inserted in the centre of the cake comes out clean. Remove from the oven and leave to cool in the cake tin.
Turn the cake out of the tin and carefully peel off the parchment paper. Slice the cake in two.
To finish: whip the cream until it holds its shape, then spread over one half of the cake. Sprinkle with half the chopped nuts and place the other half of the cake on top. Stand the cake on a serving plate.
Put the chocolate, icing sugar and water in a heatproof bowl standing over a pan of gently simmering water and heat gently until the chocolate has melted, stirring constantly with a wooden spoon. Spread the icing immediately over the top of the cake with a palette knife, then sprinkle with the remaining chopped nuts. Serve as soon as possible.
Serves 8

Caramel cream with fruits

Metric	Imperial
225 g granulated sugar	8 oz granulated sugar
300 ml water	½ pint water
600 ml milk	1 pint milk
300 ml whipping or double cream	½ pint whipping or double cream
4 eggs	4 eggs
2 egg yolks	2 egg yolks
50 g vanilla sugar	2 oz vanilla sugar

To serve:

2 oranges, peeled, divided into segments and halved	2 oranges, peeled, divided into segments and halved
100 g black grapes, halved and seeded	4 oz black grapes, halved and seeded
1 large banana, peeled and thinly sliced	1 large banana, peeled and thinly sliced

Cooking time: 1 hour 10 minutes
Oven: 180°C, 350°F, Gas Mark 4

Vanilla sugar is available in sachets from most large supermarkets and some delicatessens. Alternatively, you can make your own by burying a vanilla pod in a jar of caster sugar. Leave it for at least one week before using.

In the summer any soft fruit in season, such as strawberries or raspberries, may be used in place of those given here.

Put the granulated sugar and water in a pan and heat gently until the sugar has dissolved. Bring to the boil, then boil rapidly, without stirring, until thick and golden brown in colour.

Pour the caramel immediately into a 1 litre/2 pint ring or kugelhopf mould, tipping the mould from side to side so that the caramel covers the bottom and sides. Set aside.

Put the milk and cream in a heavy pan and bring slowly to just below boiling point. Put the eggs, egg yolks and vanilla sugar in a bowl and stir well. Stir in the scalded milk and cream, then strain the mixture into the mould.

Stand the mould in a bain marie (roasting tin half-filled with hot water), cover loosely with foil, then bake in the oven for 1 hour 10 minutes or until set. Remove the mould from the bain marie and leave until cold, then chill in the refrigerator for several hours, preferably overnight.

To serve: loosen the edge of the caramel cream with a sharp knife, then turn out on to a large deep serving dish. Mix the fruits together, then pile them into the centre of the caramel cream. Serve chilled.
Serves 8

Zabaglione

Metric	Imperial
4 egg yolks	4 egg yolks
4 × 15 ml spoons caster sugar	4 tablespoons caster sugar
4 × 15 ml spoons Marsala wine	4 tablespoons Marsala wine

Zabaglione is an Italian dessert which must be made just before serving. It is very quick and easy to make – ideal for an impromptu dinner party, but care must be taken not to let the mixture become too hot or it will curdle and not become fluffy.

Put all the ingredients in a large heatproof bowl and whisk together with a balloon whisk or rotary beater until thick and light.

Stand the bowl over a pan of gently simmering water and continue whisking until the mixture rises and becomes frothy. Pour immediately into heatproof wine glasses and serve at once with sponge fingers, ratafia biscuits or Langues de Chat (see below).

Langues de chat

Metric	Imperial
50 g butter	2 oz butter
50 g plain flour	2 oz plain flour
50 g icing sugar	2 oz icing sugar
15 g vanilla sugar (see Caramel Cream with Fruits, left)	½ oz vanilla sugar (see Caramel Cream with Fruits, left)
1 egg, beaten	1 egg, beaten

Cooking time: 4 to 6 minutes
Oven: 220°C, 425°F, Gas Mark 7

These biscuits will keep, covered tightly, for up to 2 weeks. They make a delicious accompaniment to many desserts and ice creams.

Beat the butter until soft. Sift the sugars together, then beat them into the softened butter for about 2 minutes until creamy. Slowly add the beaten egg to the mixture, beating all the time. Fold in all the flour.

Line a baking sheet with wax paper. Put the mixture into a forcing bag fitted with a small round pipe just over 5 mm/¼ inch diameter and pipe 7.5 cm/3 inch lengths on to the paper, leaving space to allow the biscuits to spread during baking. Bake in a preheated oven for 4 to 6 minutes until the edges turn golden brown. Allow to cool slightly before removing to a wire rack to cool completely.
Makes about 28

Caramel cream with fruits;
Zabaglione with Langues de chat

Scots flummery

Metric	Imperial
50 g fine oatmeal	2 oz fine oatmeal
4 × 15 ml spoons whisky	4 tablespoons whisky
2 × 15 ml spoons thick honey	2 tablespoons thick honey
300 ml double cream	½ pint double cream
4-8 shortbread fingers, to serve	4-8 shortbread fingers, to serve

Flummery is quick and easy to make; it is very rich and should be served in small wine glasses or goblets.

Put the oatmeal, whisky and honey in a heavy pan and stir well. Leave to soak for about 15 minutes, then heat gently for about 1 minute until thick, stirring constantly with a wooden spoon. Transfer to a bowl and leave to cool.

Pour the cream on to the oatmeal, then beat gently until thick and evenly blended. Spoon into 4 individual glasses, then press 1 or 2 shortbread fingers into the top of each or hand the shortbread separately. Serve chilled.

Crème pêche

Metric	*Imperial*
600 ml double cream	1 pint double cream
6 egg yolks	6 egg yolks
50 g caster sugar	2 oz caster sugar
1 ×2.5 ml spoon almond essence	½ teaspoon almond essence
100 g granulated sugar	4 oz granulated sugar
150 ml water	¼ pint water
4 large peaches, peeled, stoned and thinly sliced	4 large peaches, peeled, stoned and thinly sliced
100-175 g demerara sugar	4-6 oz demerara sugar

Cooking time: 1 hour
Oven: 150°C, 300°F, Gas Mark 2

Put the cream in a heavy pan and bring slowly to just below boiling point. Put the egg yolks, caster sugar and almond essence in a bowl and stir well, then gradually stir in the scalded cream.
Pour the mixture into a 900 ml/1½ pint round shallow baking dish, then stand the dish in a bain marie (roasting tin half-filled with hot water). Cover loosely with foil, then bake in a preheated oven for 1 hour or until set, when the centre will be as firm as jelly.
Remove the dish from the bain marie and leave until cold, then chill in the refrigerator for several hours, preferably overnight.
Meanwhile, put the granulated sugar and water in a pan and heat gently until the sugar has dissolved. Bring to the boil, then boil rapidly, without stirring, until thick and golden brown in colour. Pour immediately into an oiled shallow cake tin. Leave until set, then crack into small pieces with a rolling pin.
Arrange the peach slices on top of the baked cream, then sprinkle with the demerara sugar, covering the peaches completely. Put under a preheated hot grill for about 10 minutes until the sugar has dissolved and the juice is bubbling, then remove from the grill and leave to cool. Return to the refrigerator for about 30 minutes, then sprinkle with the chopped caramel just before serving.
Serves 6

Crème pêche; Scots flummery

Individual grape cheesecakes

Metric	Imperial
225 g plain flour	8 oz plain flour
pinch of salt	pinch of salt
50 g butter or margarine	2 oz butter or margarine
50 g lard	2 oz lard
3-4 ×15 ml spoons water	3-4 tablespoons water

Filling:	Filling:
225 g cottage cheese, sieved	8 oz cottage cheese, sieved
150 ml soured cream	1/4 pint soured cream
50 g caster sugar	2 oz caster sugar
2 eggs, beaten	2 eggs, beaten
finely grated rind of 2 lemons	finely grated rind of 2 lemons

To finish:	To finish:
100-175 g grapes, peeled, halved and seeded	4-6 oz grapes, peeled, halved and seeded
150 ml double or whipping cream	1/4 pint double or whipping cream

Cooking time: 1 hour 5 minutes
Oven: 200°C, 400°F, Gas Mark 6; reduced to
150°C, 300°F, Gas Mark 2

These pretty little cheesecakes make ideal dinner party desserts as they can be made well in advance. They also make good desserts for occasions such as buffet parties.

To make the pastry: sift the flour and salt into a bowl. Add the butter or margarine and lard in pieces, then rub into the flour with the fingertips until the mixture resembles fine breadcrumbs. Stir in the water gradually and mix to a firm dough.
Roll out the dough on a lightly floured surface and use to line 6 × 10 cm/4 inch loose-bottomed flan tins. Stand the tins on a preheated baking sheet, fill with foil and baking beans, then bake 'blind' in the moderately hot oven for 15 minutes. Remove the foil and beans, then bake for a further 5 minutes or until the pastry is set.
Meanwhile, prepare the filling: put the cottage cheese and soured cream in a bowl and beat well to mix. Stir in the sugar, then gradually stir in the eggs until evenly blended. Add the lemon rind.
Divide the filling equally between the 6 flan tins, then bake in the cool oven for 45 minutes or until the filling is risen and set.
Remove the cheesecakes from the oven and leave until cold, then remove them carefully from the tins and arrange on a serving platter. Decorate with the halved grapes, cut side down, then drizzle the cream around the grapes. Serve cold.
Makes 6 individual cheesecakes

Chocolate and rum cheesecake

Metric	Imperial
175 g plain chocolate digestive biscuits	6 oz plain chocolate digestive biscuits
75 g butter, melted	3 oz butter, melted
175 g plain chocolate	6 oz plain chocolate
2 ×15 ml spoons brandy or rum	2 tablespoons brandy or rum
2 eggs, lightly beaten	2 eggs, lightly beaten
100 g soft brown sugar	4 oz soft brown sugar
350 g full-fat soft cheese	12 oz full-fat soft cheese
2 ×15 ml spoons cornflour	2 tablespoons cornflour
a little icing sugar, sifted, to decorate	a little icing sugar, sifted, to decorate

Cooking time: 1 hour
Oven: 160°C, 325°F, Gas Mark 3

Crush the biscuits in an electric blender or between 2 sheets of greaseproof paper. Mix them with the melted butter, then press into the sides and base of a buttered loose-bottomed 18 cm/7 inch springform pan. Chill in the refrigerator for about 30 minutes until firm.
Meanwhile, break 100 g/4 oz of the chocolate into pieces, then place in a heatproof bowl with the brandy or rum. Stand the bowl over a pan of gently bubbling water and heat until the chocolate has melted.
Put the eggs and sugar in a bowl and beat together until thick. Add the cheese and continue beating until soft, then stir in the melted chocolate and cornflour until evenly blended.
Pour the mixture into the pan, stand it on a baking sheet and bake in the oven for 1 hour or until set. Remove from the oven and leave to cool, then chill in the refrigerator for at least 4 hours before serving. Remove the cheesecake from the pan and place on a serving platter. Grate the remaining chocolate and sprinkle over the top of the cheesecake, then sift over a little icing sugar. Serve chilled.
Serves 8

Individual grape cheesecakes;
Chocolate and rum cheesecake

Whisky ginger cream

This is a very quick and simple dessert to prepare for a dinner party at short notice.

Metric
2×15 ml spoons whisky
2×15 ml spoons ginger
   marmalade
finely grated rind of 1 lemon
2×15 ml spoons caster sugar
300 ml double cream,
   chilled
2 egg whites

Imperial
2 tablespoons whisky
2 tablespoons ginger
   marmalade
finely grated rind of 1 lemon
2 tablespoons caster sugar
½ pint double cream,
   chilled
2 egg whites

Put the whisky, marmalade, lemon rind and sugar in a bowl. Stir well, then leave the mixture to stand for at least 15 minutes.

Stir the cream slowly into the whisky mixture until evenly blended, then beat with an electric or rotary beater until thick.

Beat the egg whites until stiff, then fold into the cream mixture until well blended. Spoon into 4 individual wine glasses or sundae dishes, then chill in the refrigerator for at least 30 minutes. Serve chilled, with Langues de Chat biscuits (page 50) or brandy snaps.

Tarte Française; Whisky ginger cream

Tarte Française

Metric
150 g plain flour
pinch of salt
1×5 ml spoon baking
 powder
25 g vanilla or caster sugar
½ beaten egg
2×5 ml spoons milk
65 g butter or margarine

Filling:
2 large cooking apples,
 peeled, cored and sliced
25 g butter or margarine
100 g granulated sugar
1×1.25 ml spoon ground
 cinnamon
4 crisp dessert apples
juice of 2 lemons
6×15 ml spoons sieved
 apricot jam
6×15 ml spoons water
1×5 ml spoon arrowroot

Imperial
5 oz plain flour
pinch of salt
1 teaspoon baking
 powder
1 oz vanilla or caster sugar
½ beaten egg
2 teaspoons milk
2½ oz butter or margarine

Filling:
2 large cooking apples,
 peeled, cored and sliced
1 oz butter or margarine
4 oz granulated sugar
¼ teaspoon ground
 cinnamon
4 crisp dessert apples
juice of 2 lemons
6 tablespoons sieved
 apricot jam
6 tablespoons water
1 teaspoon arrowroot

Cooking time: 50 minutes
Oven: 200°C, 400°F, Gas Mark 6; reduced to
 180°C, 350°F, Gas Mark 4

To make the pastry: sift the flour, salt and baking powder into a bowl. Make a well in the centre, put in the sugar, egg and milk, then stir the ingredients together until evenly mixed. Add the butter or margarine in pieces, then work it quickly into the flour mixture using your fingers. Knead lightly to form a smooth dough, wrap in foil and chill in the refrigerator for 30 minutes.

Roll out the dough on a lightly floured surface, then use to line a 23 cm/9 inch fluted flan ring or flan dish with removable base, placed on a baking sheet. Fill the flan with foil and baking beans, then bake 'blind' in a preheated moderately hot oven for 10 minutes. Remove the foil and beans, then bake for a further 5 minutes.

Put the cooking apples in a pan with the butter or margarine, half the granulated sugar and the cinnamon. Cook over moderate heat for 10 to 15 minutes until the apples are reduced to a thick purée, stirring constantly with a wooden spoon. Spread the purée in the bottom of the flan case.

Peel the dessert apples, then slice them thinly. Arrange the slices in a circular pattern on top of the purée, overlapping them slightly. Sprinkle with half the lemon juice to prevent discolouration.

Put 2×15 ml spoons/2 tablespoons of the apricot jam in a pan with the remaining granulated sugar and 2×15 ml spoons/2 tablespoons water. Heat gently until the jam and sugar have dissolved, then boil rapidly until thick, stirring constantly with a wooden spoon. Brush the jam mixture over the apples, then bake in a preheated oven for 35 minutes, covering the edge of the pastry with foil if it becomes too brown.

Meanwhile, mix the arrowroot to a paste with a little of the remaining water. Put the remaining jam in a pan with the remaining water and lemon juice, then heat gently until the jam has melted. Stir in the arrowroot paste and bring to the boil, then continue boiling until thick, stirring constantly with a wooden spoon.

Remove the flan from the oven, then spoon the apricot glaze over the apples to cover them completely. Leave to cool. Serve cold, with whipped cream.
Serves 6 to 8

Vacherin aux marrons

Cooking time: 35 to 40 minutes
Oven: 180°C, 350°F, Gas Mark 4

Metric
4 egg whites
225 g caster sugar
1 × 2.5 ml spoon vanilla
  essence
100 g shelled hazelnuts,
  finely ground

Imperial
4 egg whites
8 oz caster sugar
½ teaspoon vanilla
  essence
4 oz shelled hazelnuts,
  finely ground

Filling:
225 g canned chestnut purée
50 g icing sugar, sifted
2 × 15 ml spoons rum
150 ml double or whipping
  cream

Filling:
8 oz canned chestnut purée
2 oz icing sugar, sifted
2 tablespoons rum
¼ pint double or whipping
  cream

To finish:
150 ml double or whipping
  cream
25 g plain chocolate,
  coarsely grated
25-50 g shelled hazelnuts,
  roughly chopped

To finish:
¼ pint double or whipping
  cream
1 oz plain chocolate,
  coarsely grated
1-2 oz shelled hazelnuts,
  roughly chopped

This type of meringue has a beautiful texture – crisp on the outside, yet soft on the inside.

Line the bottoms of 2 greased 20 cm/8 inch sandwich tins with non-stick parchment paper.
To make the meringue: beat the egg whites until stiff, then beat in the sugar a little at a time until thick and glossy. Add the vanilla essence and ground hazelnuts and fold them in gently.
Divide the meringue equally between the prepared tins and level the top. Bake in a preheated oven for 35 to 40 minutes until the meringue is crisp and lightly coloured on top. Turn out of the tins on to a wire rack, carefully peel off the parchment paper, then leave to cool completely.
Meanwhile, make the filling: put the chestnut purée in a bowl with the icing sugar and rum. Beat well until smooth. Whip the cream until it holds its shape, then fold into the chestnut mixture until evenly blended.
Place one round of meringue on a serving plate, soft side uppermost, then spread with half the filling. Place the remaining round of meringue on top, crisp side uppermost, then spread the remaining filling carefully over the centre of the cake.
To finish: whip the cream until it holds its shape, then pipe rosettes of cream around the edge of the cake. Sprinkle the chocolate over the cream rosettes, then sprinkle the chopped hazelnuts over the filling in the centre. Serve as soon as possible.
Serves 6

Linzer torte

Cooking time: 35 minutes
Oven: 190°C, 375°F, Gas Mark 5

Metric	**Imperial**
350 g frozen raspberries	¾ lb frozen raspberries
225 g caster sugar	8 oz caster sugar
2×15 ml spoons arrowroot	2 tablespoons arrowroot
2×15 ml spoons water	2 tablespoons water
3-4 ×15 ml spoons redcurrant jelly, to glaze	3-4 tablespoons redcurrant jelly, to glaze

Pastry:	**Pastry:**
175 g plain flour	6 oz plain flour
pinch of salt	pinch of salt
pinch of ground cinnamon	pinch of ground cinnamon
65 g ground almonds	2½ oz ground almonds
65 g caster sugar	2½ oz caster sugar
50 g butter or margarine	2 oz butter or margarine
1 egg, beaten	1 egg, beaten

Linzer torte; Vacherin aux marrons

Sweet almond pastry is very rich and difficult to handle, and should therefore be pressed in to the flan ring rather than rolled. Try to work in a cool kitchen with cool hands and cool utensils, and chill the dough in the refrigerator before using and baking.

To make the filling: put the raspberries and sugar in a pan, reserving 10 whole raspberries for decoration. Heat gently until the raspberries have thawed and the sugar has dissolved. Bring to the boil, then lower the heat and cook for 10 to 15 minutes until the consistency of thin jam, stirring frequently. Remove the pan from the heat.

Mix the arrowroot to a paste with the water, then stir gradually into the raspberry mixture. Return to the heat and bring back to the boil, then simmer until thick and clear, stirring constantly. Leave to cool.

Meanwhile, make the pastry: sift the flour, salt and cinnamon into a bowl, then stir in the almonds and sugar. Add the butter or margarine in pieces, then rub into the flour with the fingertips. Stir in the egg, then gather the dough together gently with the fingertips and form into a ball. Chill in the refrigerator for at least 30 minutes.

Reserve a small piece of dough for the lattice topping, then press the remaining dough into a 20 cm/8 inch plain flan ring placed on a baking sheet. Chill in the refrigerator for a further 15 minutes.

Spread the cooled raspberry mixture in the flan case. Roll out the reserved dough into strips and place across the filling in a lattice pattern, sealing the edges with water. Place the reserved whole raspberries in the 'windows' of the lattice.

Bake in a preheated oven for 35 minutes, then leave to cool on the baking sheet. Remove the flan ring carefully and transfer to a serving plate. Melt the redcurrant jelly in a small pan, brush over the top of the flan, then leave to cool.

Serve cold, with whipped cream.

Grand Marnier soufflé

Metric	Imperial
3 eggs, separated	3 eggs, separated
75 g caster sugar	3 oz caster sugar
5 × 15 ml spoons Grand Marnier liqueur	5 tablespoons Grand Marnier liqueur
1 sachet (1 × 15 ml spoon) powdered gelatine	1 sachet (1 tablespoon) powdered gelatine
4 × 15 ml spoons water	4 tablespoons water
150 ml double or whipping cream	¼ pint double or whipping cream

To decorate:

25-50 g flaked almonds, browned and left whole or finely chopped	1-2 oz flaked almonds, browned and left whole or finely chopped
1-2 oranges, peeled and sliced into thin rings	1-2 oranges, peeled and sliced into thin rings

Prepare a 13 cm/5 inch soufflé dish: cut a strip of double greaseproof paper long enough to go around the outside of the soufflé dish, overlapping slightly and 5-8 cm/2-3 inches higher than the dish. Tie securely with string, then lightly brush the inside of the paper above the rim with oil.

Put the egg yolks, sugar and Grand Marnier in a heatproof bowl standing over a pan of gently simmering water. Whisk with a balloon whisk or rotary beater until the mixture is thick and creamy, then remove the bowl from the heat and continue whisking until cool.

Meanwhile, sprinkle the gelatine over the water in a small heatproof bowl, then leave until spongy. Stand the bowl in a pan of hot water and heat gently until the gelatine has dissolved, stirring occasionally. Remove from the heat, leave to cool slightly, then stir into the egg yolk mixture.

Beat the cream until it holds its shape, then fold into the soufflé mixture. Beat the egg whites until stiff, then fold into the soufflé until evenly blended.

Pour the mixture into the prepared soufflé dish, then chill in the refrigerator for at least 4 hours or until set.

To serve: carefully remove the greaseproof collar, then brush a little more oil around the exposed edge of the soufflé. Carefully press the whole or chopped nuts around the edge, then arrange orange slices on top of the soufflé and sprinkle with any remaining nuts.
Serve chilled.
Serves 6

Almond charlotte malakoff

Metric	Imperial
1 × 600 ml packet orange or lemon jelly	1 × 1 pint packet orange or lemon jelly
150 ml boiling water	¼ pint boiling water
300 ml cold water	½ pint cold water
17 sponge fingers	17 sponge fingers
300 ml double or whipping cream	½ pint double or whipping cream
50 g ground almonds	2 oz ground almonds
a little whipped cream, to decorate (optional)	a little whipped cream, to decorate (optional)

Put the jelly cubes in a heatproof bowl, pour in the boiling water and stir to dissolve. Stir in the cold water and mix well.

Put 8 × 15 ml spoons/8 tablespoons of the liquid jelly in the bottom of a 15 cm/6 inch charlotte mould, then chill in the refrigerator until just beginning to set. (Leave the liquid jelly at room temperature.)

Dip the sponge fingers one at a time into the liquid jelly, then stand the fingers upright around the inside of the mould, pressing them gently into the base of jelly. Return the mould to the refrigerator.

Whip the cream until it holds its shape, then add the almonds and whip again. Add the liquid jelly (which should just be beginning to set) and whip into the cream until thoroughly blended.

Pour the mixture into the mould, then chill in the refrigerator overnight until set.

Just before serving, trim the ends of the sponge fingers level with the top of the mould, then dip the bottom of the mould into a bowl of hot water for a few seconds. Turn the charlotte out on to a serving plate and decorate around the top edge with whipped cream.
Serve chilled.
Serves 6

Grand Marnier soufflé; Almond charlotte malakoff

SUMMER DESSERTS

Simplicity is the keynote when making desserts in the summer, not only because the hot weather usually reduces appetites and the inclination to cook, but also because lush summer fruits are so delicious as they are, that it takes only simple additions to turn them into impressive desserts. The season for freshly picked summer fruits is short, so enjoy them at their best while you can – either just as they are, or in some of the simple ideas in this chapter.

Pears in ginger syrup

Metric	Imperial
150 ml dry white wine	¼ pint dry white wine
150 ml water	¼ pint water
4×15 ml spoons ginger wine	4 tablespoons ginger wine
100 g granulated sugar	4 oz granulated sugar
1 cinnamon stick	1 cinnamon stick
4-6 firm cooking pears	4-6 firm cooking pears
4×15 ml spoons blanched almonds, toasted, to finish	4 tablespoons blanched almonds, toasted, to finish

This dessert is best reserved for late summer and early autumn when pears are plentiful. Conference pears are ideal to use.

Put the wine, water and ginger wine in a pan with the sugar and cinnamon stick, then heat gently until the sugar has dissolved.

Meanwhile, peel the pears and cut the bottoms level so that they will stand upright. Do not remove the stalks. Stand the pears in the liquid in the pan and cook gently for about 20 minutes or until the pears are tender. Transfer the pears to a shallow serving dish, then increase the heat and boil the liquid in the pan for about 3 minutes or until syrupy.

Discard the cinnamon stick, then pour the sauce over the pears in the dish. Leave to cool, then chill in the refrigerator for at least eight hours, spooning the sauce over the pears from time to time. Sprinkle with the almonds just before serving. Serve chilled, with thin pouring cream.

Serves 4 to 6

Pavlova with tropical fruit salad

Metric	Imperial
5 egg whites	5 egg whites
350 g caster sugar	12 oz caster sugar
1×5 ml spoon vinegar	1 teaspoon vinegar
2×5 ml spoons cornflour	2 teaspoons cornflour
1×2.5 ml spoon vanilla essence	½ teaspoon vanilla essence

Topping:	Topping:
300 ml double or whipping cream	½ pint double or whipping cream
50 g vanilla sugar (page 50)	2 oz vanilla sugar (page 50)
2-3 bananas	2-3 bananas
2×5 ml spoons lemon juice	2 teaspoons lemon juice
1 fresh mango, skinned and sliced	1 fresh mango, skinned and sliced
175 g grapes, halved and seeded	6 oz grapes, halved and seeded

Cooking time: 1 hour
Oven: 230°C, 450°F, Gas Mark 8; reduced to 120°C, 250°F, Gas Mark ½

The meringue for this dessert can be made in advance and stored in an airtight tin. Do not top with the fruit until just before serving, however, or the fruit will discolour and the meringue become too soft to hold the weight of the fruit.

Draw a 23 cm/9 inch circle on a sheet of non-stick parchment paper placed on a baking sheet.

Beat the egg whites until stiff, then gradually beat in 275 g/10 oz of the caster sugar a little at a time until the mixture is thick and glossy. Beat in the vinegar, cornflour and vanilla essence. Spoon the meringue on to the circle on the parchment paper, swirling it with a palette knife to make the mixture level.

Put the meringue on the bottom shelf of the oven and immediately turn the oven down to very cool. Bake for 1 hour until crisp and firm on the outside. Remove from the oven and leave to cool, then invert the pavlova on to a serving plate and carefully peel off the parchment paper.

Whip the cream with the vanilla sugar until stiff, spread a little on the base of the meringue, then pipe the remainder around the edge of the pavlova. Peel and slice the bananas, sprinkle immediately with the lemon juice to prevent discolouration, then mix with the mango and grapes. Arrange the fruit in the centre of the pavlova and sprinkle with the remaining caster sugar. Serve immediately.

Serves 8

Pears in ginger syrup; Pavlova with tropical fruit salad

Apricot sherbet

Metric	Imperial
350 g fresh apricots, halved	12 oz fresh apricots, halved
150 ml water	¼ pint water
175 g sugar	6 oz sugar
1 × 5 ml spoon lemon juice	1 teaspoon lemon juice
300 ml double cream	½ pint double cream

Turn the refrigerator to its coldest setting. Put the apricots in a pan with their stones, the water, sugar and lemon juice. Heat gently until the apricots are soft, stirring occasionally, then remove the stones with a perforated spoon.

Transfer the apricots and liquid to a liquidizer and blend to a smooth purée. Measure the purée to 300 ml/½ pint, then leave to cool.

Whip the cream until it holds its shape, then gradually add the apricot purée, whipping constantly until evenly blended. Pour the mixture into a rigid container, then freeze in the freezing compartment of the freezer for at least 4 hours, preferably overnight.

To serve: transfer the sherbet to the main body of the refrigerator for about 10 minutes to soften slightly, then scoop into individual glasses or dishes. Serve immediately with Langues de Chat biscuits (page 50). Return the refrigerator to its normal setting.
Serves 4 to 6

Raspberry tansy omelette

Metric	Imperial
150 ml soured cream	¼ pint soured cream
2 eggs	2 eggs
75 g caster sugar	3 oz caster sugar
25 g fresh white breadcrumbs	1 oz fresh white breadcrumbs
25 g butter or margarine	1 oz butter or margarine
about 225 g fresh raspberries	about 8 oz fresh raspberries
1-2 × 15 ml spoons milk	1-2 tablespoons milk

Put about two-thirds of the soured cream in a bowl with the eggs, 50 g/2 oz caster sugar and the breadcrumbs. Beat well to mix.

Melt the butter or margarine in a 23 cm/9 inch omelette pan, then pour in the egg mixture and tilt the pan so that the mixture covers the bottom. Cook over moderate heat for 5 to 7 minutes until the underneath is set and golden brown.

Meanwhile, preheat the grill to very hot. Put the omelette under the grill and cook until the top is set and bubbling. Remove from the heat, cut into 4 wedges, then top with the raspberries. Sprinkle over the remaining sugar.

Mix together the remaining soured cream and enough milk to give a pouring consistency, then drizzle it over the raspberries. Serve immediately.

Summer peach flan

Cooking time: 20 to 25 minutes
Oven: 190°C, 375°F, Gas Mark 5

Metric	Imperial
3 eggs	3 eggs
75 g caster sugar	3 oz caster sugar
75 g plain flour	3 oz plain flour

Topping:

Metric	Imperial
2 large fresh peaches, stoned and sliced	2 large fresh peaches, stoned and sliced
3×15 ml spoons brandy	3 tablespoons brandy
2×15 ml spoons demerara sugar	2 tablespoons demerara sugar
150 ml double or whipping cream	¼ pint double or whipping cream
2×5 ml spoons caster sugar	2 teaspoons caster sugar
1×2.5 ml spoon vanilla essence	½ teaspoon vanilla essence
flaked almonds, toasted, to decorate	flaked almonds, toasted, to decorate

Apricot sherbet; Raspberry tansy omelette;
Summer peach flan

The whisked sponge base for this flan is light and airy – ideal for a summer's day. Whisked sponges stale quickly, however, and are best eaten on the day they are made. For a pretty effect, use rosy-coloured peaches and do not remove the skins.

To make the whisked sponge: line the dome of a greased 20 cm/8 inch sponge flan tin with non-stick parchment paper. Put the eggs and caster sugar in a large heatproof bowl standing over a pan of gently simmering water. Whisk with a balloon whisk or rotary beater until the mixture is thick and light and the whisk leaves a ribbon trail behind it when lifted. Remove the bowl from the heat and continue whisking until cool. Sift the flour twice, then sift half over the whisked mixture. Fold it in gently until evenly blended, then repeat with the remaining flour.
Pour the mixture into the prepared flan tin, then bake in a preheated oven for 20 to 25 minutes until the cake is springy to the touch and golden in colour. Loosen the edge of the flan with a sharp knife, then turn out on to a wire rack and leave to cool.
Meanwhile, put the peach slices in a bowl and sprinkle over the brandy and the demerara sugar.
When the flan case is cool, invert it on to a serving plate and trim the bottom edge with a sharp knife. Remove the peach slices from the liquid, then sprinkle the liquid over the flan case.
Whip the cream until it holds its shape, then add the caster sugar and vanilla essence and whip again until evenly blended. Spread the cream in the centre of the flan case, then arrange the peach slices on top. Sprinkle over the remaining demerara sugar just before serving. Serve as soon as possible.
Serves 4 to 6

Strawberry choux ring

Metric
300 ml water
100 g butter or margarine
150 g plain flour
1 × 1.25 ml spoon salt
3 eggs, beaten

Imperial
½ pint water
4 oz butter or margarine
5 oz plain flour
¼ teaspoon salt
3 eggs, beaten

Filling:
450 g fresh strawberries,
    hulled
300 ml double cream
65 g icing sugar, sifted
about 2 × 15 ml spoons
    caster sugar

Filling:
1 lb fresh strawberries,
    hulled
½ pint double cream
2½ oz icing sugar, sifted
about 2 tablespoons
    caster sugar

Cooking time: 40 to 45 minutes
Oven: 200°C, 400°F, Gas Mark 6

If the choux dough is piped in swirls on the baking sheet, the finished effect of this dessert will be really quite spectacular.

To make the choux pastry: put the water in a pan with the butter or margarine and heat gently until the fat has melted. Bring to the boil and, when bubbling vigorously, remove from the heat and immediately add the flour all at once. Beat quickly with a wooden spoon until the mixture forms a ball and draws away from the sides of the pan.
Leave the mixture to cool slightly, then beat in the eggs, a little at a time, until the pastry is smooth and glossy. Put the mixture in a piping bag fitted with a large plain nozzle and pipe a 23 cm/9 inch ring of choux dough on a greased large baking sheet.
Bake just above the centre of the oven for 40 to 45 minutes until the pastry is well risen and golden brown. Transfer to a wire rack and leave to cool.
Meanwhile make the filling: whip the cream and 50 g/2 oz of the icing sugar until thick. Chop about half the strawberries roughly, then fold into the cream.
Cut the choux ring into 6 equal portions, then slice each portion in half. Divide the strawberry cream mixture equally between each portion, then sandwich the halves together again. Re-assemble the choux ring on a serving plate, then pile the remaining whole strawberries in the centre. Just before serving, sprinkle the strawberries with caster sugar to taste and sift the remaining icing sugar over the choux ring. Serve as soon as possible.
Serves 6

Strawberry choux ring; Coeur à la crème

Coeur à la crème

Metric	Imperial
225 g full-fat soft cheese	8 oz full-fat soft cheese
pinch of salt	pinch of salt
300 ml double cream	½ pint double cream
50 g caster sugar	2 oz caster sugar
2 egg whites	2 egg whites

To finish:	To finish:
225 g fresh raspberries	8 oz fresh raspberries
4-6 × 15 ml spoons caster sugar	4-6 tablespoons caster sugar

Traditionally, Coeur à la Crème are pressed into special heart-shaped moulds, but as they are expensive to buy and sometimes difficult to obtain, it is not always possible to use them. Individual ramekin dishes make an excellent substitute.

Put the soft cheese and salt in a fine wire sieve and press through into a bowl. Whip the cream until it just holds its shape, then fold into the cheese with the caster sugar.

Beat the egg whites until stiff, then fold in until evenly blended. Put the mixture in a fine wire sieve standing over a bowl, then leave to stand in the refrigerator overnight to drain off the excess liquid.

The next day, press the mixture into 4 to 6 individual ramekin dishes and smooth the surface. Chill in the refrigerator for about 2 hours until quite firm. Just before serving, top each ramekin with raspberries and sprinkle with 1 × 15 ml spoon/1 tablespoon caster sugar. Serve immediately.

Serves 4 to 6

Gooseberry and almond soufflé

Metric	Imperial
225 g fresh gooseberries	8 oz fresh gooseberries
3 eggs, separated	3 eggs, separated
100 g caster sugar	4 oz caster sugar
1 sachet (1×15 ml spoon) powdered gelatine	1 sachet (1 tablespoon) powdered gelatine
4×15 ml spoons water	4 tablespoons water
1×1.25 ml spoon almond essence	¼ teaspoon almond essence
150 ml double or whipping cream	¼ pint double or whipping cream

To decorate:	To decorate:
about 25 g ratafias, crushed	about 1 oz ratafias, crushed
a little whipped cream	a little whipped cream

Prepare a 13 cm/5 inch soufflé dish: cut a strip of double greaseproof paper long enough to go around the outside of the soufflé dish, overlapping slightly and 5 to 8 cm/2 to 3 inches higher than the dish. Tie securely with string, then lightly brush the inside of the paper above the rim with oil.

Wash the gooseberries, then put them in a heavy pan. Cook gently for 10 to 15 minutes until the gooseberries are soft and broken up, stirring occasionally. Rub the gooseberries through a sieve, then measure 150 ml/¼ pint purée.

Put the egg yolks and caster sugar in a heatproof bowl standing over a pan of gently simmering water. Whisk with a balloon whisk or rotary beater until the mixture is thick and creamy, then remove the bowl from the heat and continue whisking until cool.

Meanwhile, sprinkle the gelatine over the water in a small heatproof bowl, then leave until spongy. Stand the bowl in a pan of hot water and heat gently until the gelatine has dissolved, stirring occasionally. Remove from the heat, leave to cool slightly, then stir into the gooseberry purée with the almond essence. Fold the purée into the egg yolk mixture until evenly blended. Beat the cream until it holds its shape, then fold into the soufflé mixture. Beat the egg whites until stiff, then fold into the soufflé until evenly blended.

Pour the mixture into the prepared soufflé dish, then chill in the refrigerator for at least 4 hours or until set.

To serve: carefully remove the greaseproof collar, then brush a little more oil around the exposed edge of the soufflé. Press the crushed ratafias around the edge, then pipe whipped cream on the top. Serve chilled.
Serves 6

Strawberry mille feuilles

Metric	Imperial
2 egg yolks	2 egg yolks
50 g caster sugar	2 oz caster sugar
scant 50 g cornflour	scant 2 oz cornflour
300 ml milk	½ pint milk

Filling:	Filling:
225 g frozen puff pastry, thawed	8 oz frozen puff pastry, thawed
150 ml double or whipping cream	¼ pint double or whipping cream
450 g fresh strawberries, hulled	1 lb fresh strawberries, hulled
1×15 ml spoon icing sugar, to finish	1 tablespoon icing sugar, to finish

Cooking time: 15 minutes
Oven: 220°C, 425°F, Gas Mark 7

To make the pastry cream: put the egg yolks in a bowl with the sugar and cornflour and stir well to mix. Scald the milk in a heavy pan, then stir gradually into the egg yolk mixture. Return the mixture to the rinsed-out pan and bring slowly to the boil, stirring constantly with a wooden spoon. Simmer until thick, then remove from the heat and leave to cool.

Meanwhile, roll out the pastry very thinly on a floured surface, then use to cover a wetted large baking sheet (about 35×30 cm/14×12 inches). Prick all over the pastry with the prongs of a fork, then bake in the oven for 10 minutes. Remove from the oven and very carefully ease the pastry away from the baking sheet with a fish slice or spatula. Turn the pastry over carefully, then return to the oven and bake for a further 5 minutes until golden brown. Transfer to a wire rack and leave to cool.

Whip the cream until it just holds its shape, then add the cold pastry cream a little at a time and continue whipping until thick and smooth. Cut 20 small strawberries in half for the topping and set aside. Mash the remaining strawberries roughly, then fold them into the cream mixture.

Cut the pastry lengthways into 3 strips, then neaten the edges. Place 1 strip on a serving plate, then spread with half the strawberry and cream mixture. Place another strip of pastry on top, spread with the remaining mixture and cover with the remaining pastry. Sift the icing sugar evenly over the pastry, then arrange the halved strawberries along the top of the mille feuilles just before serving.
Serves 4 to 6

Strawberry mille feuilles;
Gooseberry and almond soufflé

Pineapple whip

Metric
1 ripe fresh pineapple
(about 1.25 kg)
about 50 g caster sugar
2-3 × 15 ml spoons Kirsch or
brandy
about 450 ml soft-scoop
vanilla ice cream
about 2 × 15 ml spoons
chopped walnuts

Imperial
1 ripe fresh pineapple
(about 2½ lb)
about 2 oz caster sugar
2-3 tablespoons Kirsch or
brandy
about ¾ pint soft-scoop
vanilla ice cream
about 2 tablespoons
chopped walnuts

Turn the refrigerator to its coldest setting.
Stand the pineapple upright on a work surface and cut off the skin with a sharp knife, using a sawing motion and working from the top downwards. Remove the 'eyes' with the knife, then cut 6 thick slices of pineapple from the centre of the fruit. Remove and discard the centre cores and set aside the pineapple rings.
Purée the remaining pineapple flesh in a liquidizer with the caster sugar and Kirsch or brandy. (Alternatively, chop the flesh as finely as possible, then stir in the sugar and alcohol.)
Leave to stand for about 15 minutes.
Whip the pineapple quickly into the ice cream until well blended, then return to the freezing compartment of the refrigerator and chill for about 2 hours until completely firm.
To serve: allow the ice cream to soften at room temperature for about 10 minutes. Place 1 slice of pineapple on each of 6 individual dessert plates, then top with scoops of pineapple ice cream. Sprinkle with the chopped nuts and serve immediately.
Return the refrigerator to its normal setting.
Serves 6

Pineapple whip

Summer pudding

Metric	Imperial
750 g soft fresh fruit, prepared	*1½ lb soft fresh fruit, prepared*
100-175 g granulated sugar, to taste	*4-6 oz granulated sugar, to taste*
about 9 thick slices white bread from a small tin loaf, crusts removed	*about 9 thick slices white bread from a small tin loaf, crusts removed*

Summer pudding is perhaps the most delicious of all the puddings made with soft summer fruits, and it is very simple to prepare. Use a combination of fruits such as raspberries, redcurrants and blackcurrants or blackberries for a good flavour and colour, or use all one fruit, according to which is most plentiful.

Put the fruit in a heavy pan with sugar to taste and heat gently for 2 to 3 minutes until the sugar has dissolved, shaking the pan constantly. (Do not stir or overcook the fruit or it will lose its shape.) Remove from the heat and leave to cool.

Meanwhile, line the base and sides of a 900 ml/1½ pint pudding basin with bread, making sure that there are no gaps between the slices. Pour the fruit and juice into the centre of the pudding, then cover the top completely with bread and press down firmly.

Place a saucer or small plate on top of the pudding to just fit inside the basin tightly, then place heavy weights on top. Chill in the refrigerator overnight, then turn out on to a serving plate. Serve chilled, with sweetened whipped cream.

Mixed summer fruit salad; Summer pudding

Mixed summer fruit salad

Metric	Imperial
150 ml dry white wine	*¼ pint dry white wine*
150 ml water	*¼ pint water*
juice of 1 large orange	*juice of 1 large orange*
75 g caster sugar	*3 oz caster sugar*
225 g fresh strawberries, hulled and sliced	*8 oz fresh strawberries, hulled and sliced*
1 small ogen melon, skinned, seeded and diced	*1 small ogen melon, skinned, seeded and diced*
2 large fresh peaches, skinned, stoned and sliced	*2 large fresh peaches, skinned, stoned and sliced*
about 2×15 ml spoons freshly chopped mint	*about 2 tablespoons freshly chopped mint*

If you prefer a non-alcoholic fruit salad, substitute fresh orange juice for the wine. If you have a melon baller, the melon will look more attractive if scooped into neat balls.

Put the wine, water, orange juice and sugar in a pan and heat gently until the sugar has dissolved. Bring to the boil and boil rapidly for about 5 minutes or until syrupy, then remove from the heat and leave to cool. Put the fruit in a serving bowl, pour over the cool syrup, then mix together gently. Sprinkle with chopped mint and serve as soon as possible with thin pouring cream.

Mango and lemon mousse

Metric	Imperial
1 sachet (1×15 ml spoon) powdered gelatine	1 sachet (1 tablespoon) powdered gelatine
juice of 1 lemon	juice of 1 lemon
2 ripe fresh mangoes (about 225 g each), peeled and stoned	2 ripe fresh mangoes (about 8 oz each), peeled and stoned
50 g caster sugar	2 oz caster sugar
150 ml double or whipping cream	¼ pint double or whipping cream
2 egg whites	2 egg whites

Fresh peaches may be used in place of mangoes if they are unavailable, although the flavour will not be quite so distinctive. You will need 4 to 6 peaches to make up the required weight.

Sprinkle the gelatine over the lemon juice in a small heatproof bowl, then leave until spongy. Stand the bowl in a pan of hot water and heat gently until the gelatine has dissolved, stirring occasionally. Leave to cool completely.
Meanwhile, put the mango flesh and caster sugar in a liquidizer and blend to a smooth purée. Measure 300 ml/½ pint purée. Stir the cooled gelatine liquid into the mango purée, then leave the mixture until just beginning to set.
Whip the cream until it just holds its shape, then fold into the purée. Beat the egg whites until stiff, then fold in until evenly blended. Pour the mixture into a wetted 900 ml/1½ pint mould, then chill in the refrigerator overnight until set.
To serve: loosen the edge of the mousse with a sharp knife, then turn the mousse out on to a serving plate. Serve chilled.
Serves 4 to 6

Peach brûlée

Metric	Imperial
6 fresh peaches, peeled, halved and stoned	6 fresh peaches, peeled, halved and stoned
1×2.5 ml spoon ground cinnamon	½ teaspoon ground cinnamon
300 ml double or whipping cream, chilled	½ pint double or whipping cream, chilled
25 g icing sugar, sifted	1 oz icing sugar, sifted
175 g demerara sugar	6 oz demerara sugar

If you like the flavour of molasses, this simple dessert can be made with dark soft brown sugar instead of the demerara used here.

Put the peach halves, cut side down, in a single layer in a shallow heatproof dish. Sprinkle with the cinnamon. Whip the cream and icing sugar together until thick, then spread over the peaches. Sprinkle the demerara sugar over the cream to cover it completely, then put under a preheated moderate grill for a few minutes until the topping is dark and bubbling.
Remove from the heat, leave until cold, then chill in the refrigerator for at least 2 hours before serving. Serve chilled.
Serves 4 to 6

Old-fashioned junket

Metric	Imperial
600 ml fresh milk	1 pint fresh milk
1×15 ml spoon sugar	1 tablespoon sugar
1×5 ml spoon essence of rennet	1 teaspoon essence of rennet
1 egg, beaten	1 egg, beaten
1×1.25 ml spoon grated nutmeg	¼ teaspoon grated nutmeg

To make this junket a little more special, do not sprinkle with the grated nutmeg as below. Leave the junket plain until set, then cover the surface with 150 ml/¼ pint lightly whipped cream and sprinkle with the nutmeg just before serving. Junket should not be chilled in the refrigerator.

Heat the milk to blood heat (38°C/100°F), then pour into a bowl. Stir in the sugar, rennet and beaten egg, then sprinkle the top with the grated nutmeg. Cover with a clean cloth and leave in a cool place for about 1 hour until cool and set. The setting time will vary according to the room temperature and time of year. Serve at room temperature.

From the back: Mango and lemon mousse; Peach brûlée; Old-fashioned junket

WHOLESOME AND HEALTHY

If you are watching your weight, or just keeping an eye on your health in general, you will probably be denying yourself a pudding or dessert course – to avoid such fattening ingredients as sugar, pastry, chocolate and cream! Yet it's at times like these when you would like something sweet at the end of a meal, especially if the main course has been light and calorie-controlled. This chapter serves to remind you that all puddings need not be fattening or 'unhealthy', if wholesome ingredients are used with care and imagination.

Nutty meringues

Metric	Imperial
225 g light Muscovado sugar	8 oz light Muscovado sugar
4 egg whites	4 egg whites
50 g hazelnuts or walnuts, finely chopped	2 oz hazelnuts or walnuts, finely chopped
100 g plain chocolate, broken into pieces	4 oz plain chocolate, broken into pieces
2 × 15 ml spoons water	2 tablespoons water
150 ml double or whipping cream	¼ pint double or whipping cream

Cooking time: about 3 hours
Oven: 110°C, 225°F, Gas Mark ¼

Spread the sugar out over a baking sheet, then place in the oven for 15 to 20 minutes, leaving the oven door open. Remove and allow the sugar to cool so that it becomes dry and crumbly. Transfer the sugar to an electric blender and blend to a very fine powder.
Beat the egg whites until stiff, add half the sugar, then beat again until stiff. Fold in the remaining sugar with the nuts.
Pipe or spoon about 16 swirls of meringue on to parchment or waxed paper placed on baking sheets, leaving room between each swirl for expansion.
Bake in the oven for 2½ to 3 hours until the meringues are firm, leaving the oven door open for the last 15 minutes of cooking time until the meringues are completely dry. Leave to cool, then peel the paper off the meringues.
Put the chocolate and water in a heatproof bowl standing over a pan of gently simmering water and heat until the chocolate has melted. Dip half the meringues in the melted chocolate to cover the flat underside. Whip the cream until it holds its shape, then spread over the chocolate side of the meringues and sandwich them together with the plain meringues. Serve as soon as possible, while crisp.

Grapefruit and orange snow

Metric	Imperial
2 grapefruit	2 grapefruit
3 × 15 ml spoons clear honey or 2 × 15 ml spoons caster sugar	3 tablespoons clear honey or 2 tablespoons caster sugar
2 × 5 ml spoons powdered gelatine	2 teaspoons powdered gelatine
juice of 1 orange	juice of 1 orange
2 egg whites	2 egg whites

Sharp and refreshing, this fluffy dessert is fairly low in calories – ideal if you are on a diet. If you can buy pink-fleshed grapefruit, the colour of the finished dessert will be pretty and eye-catching.

Cut the grapefruit in half and scoop out all the flesh, discarding pith, pips and skin. Cut a few thin slivers of grapefruit peel with a vegetable peeler, then shred very finely. Set aside. Put the grapefruit flesh in a liquidizer with the honey or sugar and blend to a smooth purée.
Sprinkle the gelatine over the orange juice in a small heatproof bowl, then leave until spongy. Stand the bowl in a pan of hot water and heat gently until the gelatine has dissolved, stirring occasionally. Remove from the heat, then leave to cool.
Stir the cooled gelatine liquid into the grapefruit purée, then leave in a cool place until just beginning to set. Beat the egg whites until stiff, then fold into the purée until evenly mixed.
Pour the mixture into a 900 ml/1½ pint mould or 4 to 6 individual glasses, then chill in the refrigerator for at least 4 hours or until set.
Meanwhile, put the shredded peel in a small pan and cover with water. Bring to the boil and boil for 5 minutes, then drain and refresh under cold running water. Sprinkle the peel over the finished dessert just before serving.
Serves 4 to 6

Nutty meringues; Grapefruit and orange snow

Wholefood apricot crumble

Metric
225 g wild apricots or 100 g dried stoned apricots, soaked in cold water overnight
175 g demerara sugar
juice of 1 large orange
1×2.5 ml spoon ground cinnamon

Imperial
8 oz wild apricots or 4 oz dried stoned apricots, soaked in cold water overnight
6 oz demerara sugar
juice of 1 large orange
½ teaspoon ground cinnamon

Topping:
225 g plain wholewheat flour
pinch of salt
100 g margarine
50 g toasted breakfast cereal

Topping:
8 oz plain wholewheat flour
pinch of salt
4 oz margarine
2 oz toasted breakfast cereal

Cooking time: 40 to 50 minutes
Oven: 190°C, 375°F, Gas Mark 5

Wild apricots are available at most health food stores, although ordinary dried apricots may be substituted.

Drain the apricots, remove the stones, then chop the flesh roughly. Put the chopped flesh in a bowl with 100 g/4 oz of the sugar, the orange juice and cinnamon. Stir well, then place in a buttered ovenproof dish.
Put the flour and salt in a bowl. Add the margarine in pieces, then rub it into the flour until the mixture resembles fine breadcrumbs. Stir in the remaining sugar, then spoon the mixture over the apricots to cover them completely. Sprinkle the cereal evenly over the top.
Bake in the oven for 40 to 50 minutes until the topping is crisp. Serve hot with plain yogurt or thin pouring custard.
Serves 6

Apple and ginger pudding

Metric
100 g plain wholewheat flour
pinch of salt
50 g margarine
25 g wheatgerm
50 g soft brown sugar
2 eggs, lightly beaten
about 4×15 ml spoons milk
3 pieces stem ginger, finely chopped
1×15 ml spoon juice from stem ginger
2×15 ml spoons thick honey
2 medium cooking apples

Imperial
4 oz plain wholewheat flour
pinch of salt
2 oz margarine
1 oz wheatgerm
2 oz soft brown sugar
2 eggs, lightly beaten
about 4 tablespoons milk
3 pieces stem ginger, finely chopped
1 tablespoon juice from stem ginger
2 tablespoons thick honey
2 medium cooking apples

Cooking time: 30 to 40 minutes
Oven: 190°C, 375°F, Gas Mark 5

Put the flour and salt in a bowl. Add the margarine in pieces, then rub into the flour until the mixture resembles fine breadcrumbs. Stir in the wheatgerm and sugar, then the eggs and enough milk to give a soft dropping consistency. Fold in the ginger and juice until evenly blended.
Put the honey in a well-buttered ovenproof dish, then heat in the oven until melted. Meanwhile, peel, core and grate the apples.
Spread the grated apple in the bottom of the dish, then spoon the pudding mixture over the apples to cover them completely. Bake in a preheated oven for 30 to 40 minutes until well-risen and golden. Serve hot with plain unsweetened yogurt or thin pouring custard.
Serves 4 to 6

Figgy pudding

Metric	Imperial
225 g dried figs	*8 oz dried figs*
100 g self-raising flour	*4 oz self-raising flour*
pinch of salt	*pinch of salt*
100 g plain wholewheat flour	*4 oz plain wholewheat flour*
100 g margarine	*4 oz margarine*
100 g soft brown sugar	*4 oz soft brown sugar*
50 g shelled walnuts, chopped	*2 oz shelled walnuts, chopped*
1×2.5 ml spoon ground ginger	*½ teaspoon ground ginger*
2 eggs, beaten	*2 eggs, beaten*
about 2×15 ml spoons milk	*about 2 tablespoons milk*
2×15 ml spoons clear honey	*2 tablespoons clear honey*

From the back: Apple and ginger pudding; Figgy pudding; Wholefood apricot crumble

Soak the figs in cold water overnight, then drain and chop roughly.

Sift the self-raising flour and salt into a bowl, then stir in the wholewheat flour. Add the margarine in pieces, then rub into the flour until the mixture resembles fine breadcrumbs. Stir in the sugar, walnuts, figs and ginger, then stir in the eggs and enough milk to give a soft dropping consistency. Put the honey in the bottom of a well-buttered 900 ml/1½ pint pudding basin. Spoon the pudding mixture into the basin, then cover the top of the basin with greased foil. Make a pleat in the centre to allow the pudding to rise during steaming. Tie securely with string.

Place the basin in the top of a steamer or double boiler, or in a pan half-filled with gently bubbling water. Cover with a lid, then steam for 2 hours, topping up the water level in the pan as necessary.

Remove the foil from the basin, then turn the pudding out carefully on to a warmed serving dish. Serve immediately, with plain unsweetened yogurt or thin pouring custard.

Serves 6

Melon and ginger salad

Melon and ginger salad

Metric
juice of 2 oranges
3 × 15 ml spoons juice
  from stem ginger
100 g light soft brown sugar,
  or to taste
2 oranges
1 ogen melon (about 1 kg)
2 dessert apples
2 pieces stem ginger, finely
  chopped
a few fresh mint leaves or
  borage leaves, to decorate
  (optional)

Imperial
juice of 2 oranges
3 tablespoons juice
  from stem ginger
4 oz light soft brown sugar,
  or to taste
2 oranges
1 ogen melon (about 2 lb)
2 dessert apples
2 pieces stem ginger, finely
  chopped
a few fresh mint leaves or
  borage leaves, to decorate
  (optional)

This simple fruit salad is cool and refreshing. The stem ginger gives it extra bite. Use more or less sugar, according to personal taste.

Put the orange juice in a heavy pan with the stem ginger juice and sugar. Heat gently until the sugar has dissolved, then bring to the boil and boil for 5 minutes until syrupy. Remove from the heat and leave to cool. Meanwhile, peel the oranges, slice into thick rings, then cut each ring into quarters and remove any pips. Cut the melon in half, scoop out the seeds, then remove the flesh with a melon baller. (Alternatively, the flesh can be cut into small chunks with a sharp knife.) Peel and core the apples, then chop roughly. Put the fruit in a serving bowl with the ginger and sugar syrup. Stir well, then cover and chill in the refrigerator for 1 to 2 hours. Serve chilled, decorated with mint leaves, if liked.
Serves 4 to 6

Fresh lemon blancmange

Metric
4 × 15 ml spoons cornflour
50 g caster sugar
600 ml milk
1 knob of butter
finely grated rind of 1 lemon
juice of 2 lemons
few drops of yellow food
  colouring

Imperial
4 tablespoons cornflour
2 oz caster sugar
1 pint milk
1 knob of butter
finely grated rind of 1 lemon
juice of 2 lemons
few drops of yellow food
  colouring

Most children like blancmange, and it's a quick and easy dessert to prepare for them at teatime. The tangy taste of blancmange made with fresh lemons is particularly good.

Mix the cornflour and sugar to a paste with a little of the milk in a large heatproof bowl. Heat the remaining milk to just below boiling point, then stir gradually into the cornflour paste. Return the mixture to the rinsed-out pan, bring to the boil, then lower the heat. Add the butter and simmer for 3 minutes until thick, stirring constantly.
Remove from the heat and leave to cool for a few minutes, then add the lemon rind and gradually stir in the lemon juice and food colouring until they are evenly blended.
Pour the blancmange into a wetted 600 ml/1 pint mould, leave until cold, then chill in the refrigerator until set. Serve chilled.

Orange and yogurt jelly

Metric
4 large oranges
150 ml water
100 g caster sugar
1 sachet (1×15 ml spoon)
  powdered gelatine
juice of 1 lemon
150 ml plain unsweetened
  yogurt

Imperial
4 large oranges
¼ pint water
4 oz caster sugar
1 sachet (1 tablespoon)
  powdered gelatine
juice of 1 lemon
¼ pint plain unsweetened
  yogurt

To decorate:
2 small oranges, peeled and
  sliced into rings
25-50 g almonds, slivered or
  chopped (optional)

To decorate:
2 small oranges, peeled and
  sliced into rings
1-2 oz almonds, slivered or
  chopped (optional)

Remove the rind from the oranges with a vegetable peeler, then put them in a pan. Squeeze the juice from the oranges and measure 300 ml/½ pint, making up the volume with water if necessary. Pour the orange juice into the pan, add the water and sugar and heat gently until the sugar has dissolved. Bring slowly to the boil, then remove from the heat and leave to infuse for at least 10 minutes.

Meanwhile, sprinkle the gelatine over the lemon juice in a small heatproof bowl, then leave until spongy. Stand the bowl in a pan of hot water and heat gently until the gelatine has dissolved, stirring occasionally. Strain the orange juice mixture to remove the rind, then stir in the gelatine liquid. Leave until cold, then stir in the yogurt. Pour into a wetted 600 ml/1 pint mould, then chill in the refrigerator for at least 4 hours or until set. Turn the jelly out on to a serving platter and decorate with orange rings and nuts, if using. Serve chilled.

Fresh lemon blancmange; Orange and yogurt jelly

Index

ACKNOWLEDGEMENTS

The publishers would like to thank Tefal Housewares Limited for their help in the preparation of this book.

The publishers would like to thank the following companies for their kindness in providing materials and equipment used in the photographs for this book.

Elizabeth David, 46 Bourne Street, London SW1: pages 48, 49 white china goblets; 66, 67 coeur à la crème pots (white china); 73 and title page white ceramic spoons, and title page white ceramic bowl. Conran Shop, 77-79 Fulham Road, London SW3: contents page, white stem glasses and silver rim coffee cups.

We should also like to thank the following:

Photographer Bryce Attwell with stylist Roisin Nield: all prelims and pages 6, 7, 10, 11, 14, 15, 17, 19, 20, 21, 22, 30, 32, 33-79.

Photographer Paul Williams with stylist Penny Markham: cover photograph and pages 8, 9, 12, 13, 23, 24, 25, 26, 27, 28, 29, 31.